Trevor
FIVE OWLS
STORIES FROM NATURE

Trevor Beer's
FIVE OWLS
STORIES FROM NATURE

HALSGROVE

Originally published by Halsgrove, 2007

Copyright © 2007 Trevor Beer

All rights reserved. No part of this publication may be reproduced, stored in a retrieval system, or transmitted in any form or by any means without the prior permission of the copyright holder.

British Library Cataloguing-in-Publication Data
A CIP record for this title is available from the British Library

ISBN 978 184114 671 3

HALSGROVE
Halsgrove House
Ryelands Farm Industrial Estate
Bagley Green, Wellington, Somerset TA21 9PZ
Tel: 01823 653777   Fax: 01823 216796
email: sales@halsgrove.com
website: www.halsgrove.com

Printed in Great Britain by Cromwell Press Ltd

Contents

	Introduction	7
1	Mist - The Story of a Barn Owl	9
2	Athene - The Little Owl	57
3	Strix - The Tawny Owl	79
4	Asio & Hootlet	107
5	Flammeus & Shade	117

Dedicated to Grail, the little owl who lived with us for three years, found as an orphan, and to Woody, a tawny owl brought to me injured, and who stayed to charm us with its beauty, and to all the other owls I have looked after and released over many years of caring for sick and injured wildlife.

Introduction

Owls are fascinating birds. Whatever it is about them, whether it is in their facial expressions as we see them, or their mainly nocturnal activities, their strange cries when hunting or during the breeding season, their very mix of differences and similarities to ourselves as we perceive them, indeed all of these things, and so much more that comes from their seemingly mysterious ways, it makes them 'OWLS'... magical birds, and these five tales of the British owl species will hopefully leave the reader knowing far more about them and our relationships with them. This book is dedicated to owls everywhere, and to everyone who loves owls for as we continue to pressurise planet Earth it is only our love for wild creatures that will help them to survive.

Trevor Beer MBE
North Devon

Trevor Beer's FIVE OWLS

1
Mist - The Story of a Barn Owl

Prologue

I have grown up in the barn owl country of North Devon, seeing times when the species was common in the 1940s and 50s, to a decline so notable as to be alarming by the 1980s and into the 21st century.

Pollution, habitat loss, road deaths, all have contributed to the decline of this wonderful owl but interestingly, as I write this on Halloween, 2002, I am hopeful that the barn owl is making a comeback for I have seen more about these past two years than for a long time.

The story of Mist the Barn Owl is a true one in that, as with 'Old Red' my story of a Devon fox, I have brought together a number of observations and linked them as the life of one barn owl. It is a fact that shortly after the young Mist left the Derby Yeo area, an owl did turn up at my privately owned nature sanctuary at East Down, just as in the story. It could have been, may well have been, the very same bird. Also the luminosity from honey tuft fungi is quite correctly described and it will rub off on contact to produce the effect referred to in the story.

Chapter 1. The Beginning

Alba the Barn Owl had lived along the green, lushly wooded valley of the Yeo River since she had first hatched some two years before in a large, old whitewashed mill building that had once seen trains go by on the narrow gauge railway between Barnstaple and Lynton towns.

Though the railway had closed in 1935 locals still called the walk along this river bank 'Derby Line' almost 70 years later, Derby being an area of dwellings, shops and pubs on the outskirts of the Market town of Barnstaple, that kept itself to itself almost as a separate village.

Indeed men and women still live at Derby who could recall the old 'Puffing Billy' train labouring on its twenty miles journey to Lynton and told tales of how, on the steep inclines, they would jump down from the carriages, pick a bunch of flowers and get back on again!

In those days the countryside was far richer in wildlife than today, with barn and tawny owls a common sight tolerated and left to their own devices as 'good for us to ev about'...

And Alba's ancestors had lived in hollow trees along the river Yeo Valley and elsewhere in the countryside long before that time, long before the mill was built, before even mankind had come to settle, to fell woodlands or to farm the land.

From that time the white owls had begun to use the buildings of man, even when he brought his livestock into the same dwellings in winter, before farms became with separate dwellings for man and his beasts, and barns for cattle, sheep and crops were built for their particular purposes.

And so the white owls which killed rats and other creatures which lived off man's crops and seeds, became the Barn Owls and a friend of the farmers, and of all country people.

Alba was now two years from her fledging in the mill building. Here she and five brothers and sisters had hatched on a bed of straw and old hessian sacks on the upper floor of a room with a small access window high above the axle and remains of a water wheel which had once driven the mill machinery, powered by water flowing along the Yeo leat and under-shooting the wheel.

Alba had flown from the mill building with her family one summer's evening when buttercups carpeted the valley fields and a setting sun sent long tree shadows reaching towards Exmoor. Her first perch in the new world of her strengthening wings beyond the mill was the iron railing of an old plank bridge over the Yeo waterway. She had scrabbled to gain her balance and foothold then watched her brothers and sisters flying about the field after their mother. Alba's father had perched beside her then, overlooking a pair of mallard with six downy young. They watched the ducks swimming in the ripples and dapples of sunlight glints on water until the fading light sent them beneath the single arch to their night roost.

The water glints, golden lit by the setting sun, flickered and rippled with the movement caused by the gentle wakes of the duck and drake mallard by Roth's Mill, as the old whitewashed building was called. By the derelict water wheel axle and cog, now rusty and held rigid by age in old stonework that had once supported the timber undershot mill wheel that drove the mill machinery, mallard had made their homes for many years.

Just upstream the six mallard ducklings rested silently beneath bushes by a tiny bridge with a single arch, watching their parents swim towards them, to waddle onto the grass sward and settle beside them for the night to come. Their dark eyes closed as they huddled together, downy bodies warming each other. The female mallard lay close against them and uttering a soft bubbling call tucked her head beneath one wing, feeling her mate warm beside her, and she fell asleep.

A hundred human paces along the lane which ran by the old mill a dog fox picked up a hen from where it dozed, warmed by a stone wall. The hen squawked once in protest, buffeting the face of the fox with one wing as she died in his jaws. The fox was Old Red who lived over the hill in the Bradiford Valley. An opportunist hunter he now loped back into Raleigh Road to make his way homeward with his prize as tiny feathers drifted in the breeze from the west and fell into the Yeo leat as the sun finally set and darkness fell upon the valley.

Then Alba flew with her father to explore the sounds of voles and mice squeaking shrilly in long grass and wildflowers about the field edge, Alba learning the hunting skills of her kind for the coming time of fending for herself, for the family life of owls, spent together as adults and young, is short compared to that of human-kind.

Chapter 2

Two years had passed by, two summers and winters during which Alba had hunted the valley, eventually moving up river from the old mill to find her independence at Yeo farm just two miles from the place of her birth. Here the hunting was easy, small mammals plentiful and Alba had known only one hard winter period when snow and ice had brought hunger and much daylight hunting but she had survived the bleak coldness of the time which fortunately was brief and followed by mild days of recovery.

It was now June and Alba peered from the barn window where she had lived for the past two years, watching her mate flying towards her over the field where Ruby Devon cattle dozed, glowing red in the light from a setting sun. She had taken a mate for the first time some months before and now she was perched on the barn loft window-sill with her own four young behind her eager to test their wings. They had flown from beam to beam in the large loft for some days and were now ready for the great outdoors.

Alba had laid four eggs at two day intervals, incubating from the first egg for just over four weeks, watched over by her mate who brought food caught in the vicinity of Yeo Farm and the next farm along the valley. For nine weeks from the eggs hatching the two adult owls had hunted to supply the nestlings and themselves with food, occasionally watched by the farm owner and his wife, delighted to have breeding barn owls on site after a lapse of several years.

The farmer had seen two owls carrying food into the barn one evening, realising for the first time that there must be young in the loft. He had been used to seeing Alba about but so unobtrusive had she been for many days that he had not been aware of two birds being present. On one sunny day he had gone quietly into the barn to hear the strange snoring note of the young owls.

"Just like the sound of the distant waves on a shingle beach", he had told his wife. She, too, had gone to listen and then they had left the owls in peace, leaving the barn door open as they did at the swallows returning to nest in the lower room of the barn, as bluebells carpeted their oak woodlands each year.

Lesser celandines, primroses and violets, wood anemones and bluebells, all had bloomed and gone over for another year and now it was once again the time of buttercups, with cow parsley still showing in clouds of frothy bloom since April, along the hedge banks and lanes. Fairy Lace and Queen Anne's Lace the farmer's wife called it, her husband speaking of it as Hedge Parsley.

He was gladdened by the presence of barn owls on the farm for the species was said to be in decline. A pair of barn owls would, with the resident vixen and other predators about the valley, kill "the bleddy rats" that were on the increase and had been, he'd observed, for three or four years. A few rats could be expected on most farms at some time but he did not like the notable increase, putting it down to their resistance to poisons, warmer winters and a slight decline in predators which he, as a countryman born and bred found disturbing. But barn owls yes, good news for the farm, perhaps a good omen after a year of foot and mouth disease worries and the plethora of paper work so much part of the farmers' lot these days.

But Alba, who knew nought of such matters, launched from her loft window sill perch to wing silently out onto the branch of an oak tree close to the barn building as the eldest by days of her four young came to perch on the sill she had just vacated.

The eldest young owl, a female, watched her mother fly out onto the oak branch, wanting to follow her, seeing her father patrolling the field beyond in low flight. Behind, her two brothers and a sister jostled to be next to the window opening, each eager now to explore the world beyond the barn.

Just weeks before they had been blind, naked and helpless, totally reliant on their parents, Alba feeding them and their father bringing food in the claws of one foot, always in line with his body. He would then perch on the oak branch to transfer the food to his beak, then fly in to the nest chamber to give it to Alba to feed the chicks.

If her young did not accept the food offered them Alba gave a chittering call to tell them food was available. They would then utter squeaking, hoarse calls in begging fashion and Alba would feed them, looming over them protectively whilst doing so.

And so it was that the young owls had grown from blind nakedness to strong, healthy owls more or less the image of their parents save for some down remaining here and there. As they became able to fly so they had played hunting games, pouncing on owl pellets, rustling leaves and beetles. Once the eldest pounced awkwardly onto a mouse that had dared to cross the loft floor and killing it by direct hit she had remained guarding it, staring down at her first real prey until Alba's arrival at the window caused her to eat hurriedly.

One evening when the 'pink-pink' clamour of blackbirds going to roost was loud upon the air Alba perched very still on the oak branch her mate had always used to transfer prey from claws to beak. She watched the valley for a long while until the man walking with his border collie came out of the weir field to disappear from sight along the lane.

Then she screeched once with a strange shortened note, her eldest daughter promptly responding by flapping her wings and falling from the sill. Almost at ground level she flapped harder, sending scores of whirling gnats soaring all ways, finding she was suddenly half way across the field, her father flying beside her. Excited and confused, seeing her father flying ahead to turn, she crash landed on the ground amidst meadow buttercups.

Righting herself she stared about, seeing the now darkening shadow of the barn and one of her brothers flying towards her. Within the hour, as a full moon rose to turn the landscape silver with her light, all four young were winging about the field watched by the two adult barn owls.

"Looks as if all's well Mary", the farmer said to his wife as they watched from an upstairs window of their own dwelling. "I reckon them owls'll do alright, specially with this drop of fine weather we're having".

"Yes dear. I think you're right. Let's just hope they all find homes later on and that the breeding pair stay with us. That'd be good".

Moving On.
In the second week of the fledging of the four young barn owls, in which they no longer regarded the nest site as their only home, there came about a week of stormy winds and rain. The four young owls had occasionally returned to the farm barn to be fed but gradually the situation had changed. Alba,

whose roost and chosen breeding site it was, became restless for her mate once more for barn owls sometimes raise two broods in a year and she was young and healthy.

One of the brothers had already moved on, perhaps unwittingly for he had followed Alba upstream along the Yeo one night and in turning away towards Shirwell village had lost sight of his mother. Thus his independence had been thrust upon him and he was soon hunting the area of the old churchyard, hunting and haunting the area to the delight of village locals.

With the coming of the week of rain the oldest young owl had roosted one night on the interior beam of a linhay two fields from the farmhouse, flying inside as a sudden squall of hail swept along the valley. There she shook icy raindrops from her feathers and preened as the night grew dark and clouds obscured the moon.

The next morning she awoke with a start to see two rats in the dawn light wandering into the linhay and along an inner wall whereupon she dropped silently upon the smaller of the two. With vice-like squeezing talons she took the life from the brown rat, the other squealing with fear as it ran from the sheltering linhay. She tore and ate, suddenly aware that she was able to take her own food. She gazed about the linhay taking in every detail, the open front of the red tiled building, the earth floor, the beams for perching and outside, a paddock field with nettles and grassland, where a brown pony bought from Exmoor was grazing quietly.

The owl dropped her head to her breast and dozed, her white disc face beautiful in the sunlight, the tail of the brown rat hanging down from her beak and she fell asleep.

That evening on awakening she stared down at the linhay floor, regurgitating a pellet of rat fur and bones onto the ground below. She stretched her wings wide as owls need to do as part of warming up, as part of being a barn owl, warming up for the world of flight, an important moment in her life.

She was now a lone barn owl, a learning adult bird, her brief origins in the Yeo Farm barn behind her and once again the moon rose as darkness fell to erase the dimmity from the land.

Chapter 3

The month of June passed swiftly for the young owl, Midsummer's longest day a time of fox cubs learning to hunt with their mother, watched by the barn owl as she roosted by day in an old shippon no longer used by cattle. The foxes would appear in the evening time, running in line behind the vixen at the lower edge of an ancient pack horse route called Smokey House Lane. The owl was used to foxes. She had met with many on her travels about the valley at night paying them no real heed, though twice she had caught rats put out of the lane at night by their hunting.

The fox earth was in a quarry along the lane, called Smokey House from charcoal burning fires of a century or more ago. The owl had hunted there a few times, taking mice and voles. Once she had eaten beetles from the carcase of a wood pigeon and learning, she had turned over many a carcase for its beetles though she was no carrion eater. Some vague stirrings in Mist's memory caused her to recall taking food to the barn floor for her youngest brother who fell from the loft in a rough and tumble one day. She and her sisters fed him as their parents brought food, though the other male sibling ignored these proceedings and never assisted.

And so June passed into July and for a while the owl had found the living was easy from the old shippon. Occasionally, on nights when she was not hunting she would lean back against the shadowy wall just inside her exit and entrance window as a human came quietly to take items from a cavity in the wall. The man was a poacher, the cavity his hiding place for snares he used in his trade for he took no items home with him in case he was apprehended by water bailiffs or landowners. On one rainy night when the poacher was forced to wait out heavy storm conditions he sat in a dry corner of the shippon grinning up at the owl, enjoying her company, knowing of her presence and that she too was waiting to hunt for food as was he.

Bill Shapland, known as 'Shappy' to his friends in the area of pre-war houses known as Derby, at the edge of Barnstaple, was over 60 years of age but looked much younger. He was a local man of local descent, his father killed during World War II when he was at school. Brought up with two brothers and two sisters by his mother he had 'roughed it' along the rivers and streams catching fish, pheasants and rabbits so that there was always food on the table. At 18 he had been called up for National Service in the Army, learning skills with R.E.M.E, that had brought him to working in a local garage as a vehicle mechanic on his return home. He had worked hard, earning as much by moonlighting, repairing vehicles 'on the side', as at work in the garage. His home was in a terrace of houses comfortably immaculate, paid for and owned by he and his wife who was also of local stock. They had no children. 'Us ev tried but twasn't to be', he'd said many times. Now his wife contented herself with her home, two cats and helping with Shappy's homing pigeons in excellent housing at the end of their vegetable and flower garden.

But instilled within him was Shappy's hunter, gatherer, younger days and he could not resist a couple of nights each month picking up some free food in the countryside he knew as well as anyone and better than most.

"Don't belong to anyone. Tis there to feed us if us takes the trouble to ketch it", he'd be heard to say in the local pub just along the road from where he had gone to school. He and his wife Wendy, still an attractive woman of just over 50, were Saturday night regulars at the local, now somewhat isolated in a road that had seen much demolition for so-called council 'slum clearance' when in fact the houses were well maintained and better built than much of the council housing that took their place.

"Just a money making dodge by the council", Shappy would say. "Kicking us out of our homes to go into theirs and pay rent to them. Not me. Bought me own place." He would say this proudly over his pint of best bitter, then talk of 'the old days' as if they were centuries ago. His wife Wendy would grin and sip her glass of gin and tonic, a weekend treat though her much loved husband had always been an excellent provider, her own income at the local 'lace factory' saved for a rainy day.

And now Shappy was sitting hunched against the wall watching the barn owl above his head.

"You'm like mist boy. Or be ee a maid I wonder? Well then I'll call ee Mist so as it don't matter one way or t'other. That's my name for ee so that's your name."

The owl gazed down at him head on one side, watching, listening to the sounds issuing from the man's mouth, not understanding, yet feeling no fear of this creature in the corner of the old building any more than she feared cows or sheep.

After an hour had passed the storm which had come unexpectedly along the valley ceased as suddenly as it had begun, a last buffeting of wind driving the rain clouds further inland onto Exmoor. Silver blue light penetrated into the barn for an almost full moon, no longer obscured by clouds, bathed the land in its light. Shappy rose, rubbing his cramped knees, feeling the pins and needles of circulation restored as he turned his back on Mist to gaze out across the fields, considering what to do next.

He jumped, startled, as Mist flew on silent wings to pass his head to begin quartering the sodden grassland.

"You'll find nort worth the taking there my beauty", he called after the barn owl. "Too early I reckon, nort much'll move in this wet". He watched the owl fly low along the high hedge row, the moonlight bathing her body silvery white, then she went up and over into the next field and was gone from sight. He felt pleased he had thought to name the bird.

Shappy looked down at his boots bought from the Army & Navy Surplus Stores at the edge of town, wishing he could fly like an owl as out he went into the yielding mud and grass. He grinned to himself, knowing his own chances of a find were about nil and he had two fields and a muddy lane to walk before he would find tarmac beneath his feet. He'd told his wife he could smell rain in the air. She said stay home then. Then the TV forecast had said 'tomorrow', so here he was about to take home muddy feet and trousers. Time to pack it in and retire, he thought.

Muttering to himself as he crossed the fields to the lane he glanced at his luminous dial watch. Time to pick up fish and chips to take home for Wendy and himself, and a treat for the cats, Shappy thought. Then startled he came face to face with the barn owl on the stile at the lane edge. Mist held a rat in her beak, caught in the lane moments before. Even as he stared she flew with her capture, up and over his head to fly off in the direction of the barn, a white ghostly shape in the moonlight.

Shappy gave the departing owl a thumbs up signal and chuckling he went cheerfully homeward with a story to tell over a fish and chip supper.

Chapter 4

August, harvest time, the first blackberries ripe on brambles following a period of sunshine and rain. Mist moved her roosting between the linhay and a hollow ash at the edge of woodlands upstream of the building. She used the linhay often by night but by day she sometimes left to avoid youngsters on school holidays for they used the building as their den on dry days and were noisy in their play.

Shappy had now retired from his garage work, content to take on private vehicle repairs in his own time. He had the use of a builders yard for his work, the rent being to keep the builder's two vehicles and family cars in good repair. He obtained a lurcher, a greyhound, collie cross a fine dog of dark grey hue which blended with the night. He had held to his decision to give up his poaching forays and instead had obtained permission to do a bit of rabbiting at two farms along the Yeo, the one where Mist lived and the farm further up stream. Both owners had known Shappy for years and knew of his occasional night time jaunts. But their only argument against poachers was of the modern kind who travelled in gangs, usually townies seeking big money. Shappy did not bother the farmers, who had told him some years past that if he got himself caught by the local water bailiffs when after a salmon then that was for him to sort out.

Now they were happy to give him rabbiting access over their land, amused that he had 'retired'. In fact Shappy had quietly and shyly asked Wendy to make his August birthday present a "pair of they binoculars", for he was going to watch the wildlife more closely.

She had done so gladly, pleased to see her husband changing course as she had always secretly worried at his night time jaunts even though she knew he could look after himself well enough. She had smiled when he said he wanted a pair of binoculars to fit in his pocket, "or the gang down the pub will rib me something chronic", he'd said, if they saw him wandering about with a big pair round his neck. Shappy had finally decided for a high powered monocular which slipped easily into his pocket and was delighted with the sharp image he received when watching a kingfisher at Derby weir, the first time he used it.

On a mild evening at the end of August Shappy and his wife, who had become fond of the lurcher they had 'rescued' from the local Canine Defence League kennels, were out walking the fields by the linhay farm, for she had asked to be shown 'the owl'.

"Evening Shappy, Mrs Shapland. Nice dog you've got there", the farmer said, eyeing Bramble appreciatively, then, "how do you fancy a couple of days work Shappy, for me like, cash on the nail?"

"Sounds fine by me," Shappy replied. "Is the Land Rover playing up?"

"Oh no. Running sweet as a nut, always does. No this isn't vehicles. Best come in and have a cuppa. Kettle's on for one, soon's I get back home".

Shappy and his wife exchanged glances. They had not been asked in to the farm before but then, the two of them were not usually out in the fields together.

"Bring the dog too, he wont hurt", the farmer said, "I'm muddier than him".

Indoors they sat in the huge kitchen diner of the old farmhouse as the farmer introduced his wife, Lin, and said they were to call him Jack. Mugs of strong tea were placed before them as Bramble was treated to several ginger snap biscuits much to his delight.

"Now then Shappy", Jack said, "Down to business. You know the old linhay in the cleave, where you used to leave bits and pieces?"

Shappy reddened and nodded. "Yes, course I do. I ducked in there a lot when twas raining. You've got a barn owl down there you know."

Jack nodded. "Yes, but I only knew come a week or so ago. Went down to see what those kids might have been up to and found a few comics and a couple of sticks they play with, then saw the owl watching me. It didn't fly away, must have thought twas you."

Shappy grinned. "Might've done. It got used to me about. Don't know if'n it's boy or maid, so called'n Mist". He reddened again. "Well it looked like a mist gwane across the fields so that's why I called'n it."

"Perfect name", said Lin. "That's what I'd have called it".

"Well now", Jack said. "Trouble is I found lots of the tiles are loose and the back wall hidden by the ivy is only held up by the stuff and that elder tree that grows against it. Another year and twill be falling down, or worse those kids will cause it then there'll be an awful accident. Us don't want that Shappy." He looked at his wife who nodded worriedly.

"No, can't have that. Like Jack says tis held up more by luck than ought else," Lin agreed.

"So us wondered, now you'm not down the garage like, if you'd fancy taking the whole thing down and what to do with the stones and that? Take as long as you like and see that owl's alright in the bargain."

Shappy drank from his mug, ideas already in his mind.

"Yes Jack. I'll do it. I'll enjoy it. All I'll need's the tools and a barrow, oh and a tea chest and one of they builders pallet things." He grinned at their mixed glances of pleasure and puzzlement.

"I've got all the tools and a wheel barrow Shappy. No problem. Just come and help yourself. But a tea chest and pallet. Not for carrying the stones surely?"

"No". Shappy warmed to his new task even as he sat talking. "Tea chest on to a pallet, up in your barn, make a lovely platform and nest box for barn owls. A chap who writes about nature in the local paper told me he's had success with it several times, so worth a try wouldn't ee say? I could even get'n to come along I'm sure".

Jack nodded eagerly. "Sounds good to me. And even better perhaps. I have two big beer barrels, the wooden ones, in the barn. You could use one of those if you like".

"Yes. That'd be ideal. And I could cart all the stones down yer to the garden and build a walled, waist high flower bed onto your existing wall out there. Use up the stones nicely I reckon."

"Oh yes!" Lin exclaimed. "But for a herb garden. What a great idea. I love herbs. You can always come and pick some Wendy. Let's do it all and the tiles will always come in handy".

"That's settled then". Jack sighed happily. Stay sitting down and I'll pour us a glass of something stronger. 'Water of Life' alright for everybody?" He pointed to a bottle of malt whisky on a huge sideboard.

"Sounds good to me folks", chuckled Shappy as Bramble came to put his chin on his knee. "Sounds really good".

Chapter 5

It was the first day of September and Mist was dozing after a night of hunting which eventually proved fruitful as she caught three wood mice close to the linhay entrance. Her summer had been one of many wood mice for the two adjoining landowners had cut hay at different times. Thus Mist had enjoyed catching as many as four mice in a quarter of an hour, then she rested with two of these on her linhay perch beside her. She had swallowed the other two whole, as is the way of barn owls. Now in her resting she would digest the flesh, then regurgitate the fur and bones in a compact pellet, large, black and glossy pellets of unwanted parts of her prey.

Mist was not to know but on one of the days of children visiting the linhay, two boys had collected eight of her pellets, taking them away in a plastic bag with much excitement. The boys were keen on nature study and had dissected the barn owl pellets to glue the remains of small mammals on to cards bought for the purpose. They were for their nature table at school on their return. Skulls, sternums, jaw bones, vertebrae and ribs, even the beak of a small bird they had found and carefully labelled so as to know what barn owls eat.

Now Mist heard footfalls coming nearer towards the linhay and the panting, snuffling sounds of a dog. Into the linhay came the dark, agile shape of Bramble who peered up at her with large brown eyes, then the dog began to snuffle at the pellets beneath her perch.

Leaning forward Mist opened her wings and swooping flew out from the linhay entrance just as Shappy arrived, one wing brushing his cheek as she flew into the bright daylight. Shappy watched her circle the linhay then fly higher to head across the field in the direction of the woods on the hillside.

He muttered an exclamation, feeling upset at seeing he had disturbed the owl from its roosting and moreso that the bird flew away from the direction of the farm. He had spent the day before fixing up the nest box on its pallet platform with the help of a local naturalist and was pleased with the result. The naturalist had told him that if barn owls were about then with a bit of luck the box, or barrel as it was, may well be accepted but not to expect immediate miracles. Sometimes it all happened quickly, sometimes it might take a year or two. He himself had various nest boxes up, some used, some including a barn owl box high in a tree, still unused.

Shappy went back outside to the wheel barrow he had trundled over the field, putting out a sledge hammer as the farmer arrived with a metal ladder and tool box in the rear of his Land Rover. Even as he was driving away again Shappy was climbing the ladder to begin the task of removing the loose tiles from the linhay roof. Mist's home of many months would soon be but a memory in the landscape.

That same night a rising moon saw Mist leave the ash tree hollow to fly across the field to her favourite perch on the linhay beam. She looked about her, then upwards to the heavens, seeing the sky, the moon and stars instead of her usual welcoming darkened abode. A gust of wind from the south-west stirred the elder tree behind the linhay, rustling its leaves, bringing the first heavy drops of rain across the already glistening town rooftops to reach the field. Mist felt the raindrops beating down upon her. Looking skywards once more she flew up and through the gaping hole that was once the roof, then circling the neat pile of old tiles upon the grass she flew rapidly towards the nearby woodland edge lit by the moon shining on the white trumpets of great bindweed flowers and the round fruits of snowberry paler even than she.

With a flurry of wings she landed upon an ash tree branch then shaking herself free of rain water she went into the dry, comforting shelter of the hollow she knew so well, to perch listening to the rain. Hungry but dry, Mist knew there would be no hunting this night and she was soon asleep.

In the warmth of his bed Shappy put aside the book he was reading. Getting out of bed so as not to disturb his wife he closed the window against the beating rain. He sighed deeply, thinking of Mist, wondering how the barn owl was faring, then patting Bramble who lay on a rug at the foot of the bed he climbed back in, turned off the bedside lamp and fell asleep.

Chapter 6

September moved into October, the rainy beginning to the autumn making way for an 'Indian Summer' with sunshine following misty mornings.

Mist hunted the fields and wood edge mostly at dusk and dawn, catching small mammals with ease. Occasionally she would hunt late into the night when foxes and badgers were about, sometimes seeing a poacher or two when the salmon were running, penetrating the Yeo River as their ancestors had done for thousands of years before them. She saw, too, a man with a darkly grey dog often walking the fields, sometimes catching the rabbits which ran into brambles and gorse, rabbits too large for her to catch. Once they sat against the old elder tree where her linhay shelter used to stand but there was little sign of it now save for bare soil patches already grassing over.

On that evening Mist was perched unseen above them, well hidden by the elder leaves already in autumn colours. She often perched here for the tree afforded her views along the hedge where field and bank voles were usually plentiful.

Mist's sharp black talons gripped the tree branch as she watched the dog and human below. The man leaned forward suddenly, picking an object from the ground. He gazed at it then looked up directly at where she perched invisible to him. She could see his eyes moving, staring and then he turned back to look at the object in his hand.

"Cor look at this Bramble. Tis a barn owl pellet and tis a fresh one no more'n a day or so old I'd say. That Mist is still about". The lurcher sniffed at the pellet of tiny mammal remains then resumed chewing grasses as he often did when his owner paused for a while on their regular walks.

"I'm gwane to take this home and keep it in a jam jar in the shed as a keep sake", Shappy told his dog.

And tomorrow I must ask Jack and Lin if they see much of the barn owl. They'd have said if it was roosting in the barrel nest box, he thought to himself. A contented man was Shappy but he felt suddenly warmer inside as he realised Mist remained about. He rose deciding the grass was becoming too heavy with dew.

"God I'm stiff's a poker Bramble. Let's walk up to the weir and take a look see, then us'll go home and put our feet up boy".

The lurcher wagged his tail, always preferring to be on the

move as all good country dogs are. Shappy strolled along the river bank, the barn owl pellet safe in his pocket. Suddenly he was gazing up at the deeply rich redness of the haws along the hedge and deciding when to come back and pick the sloes, ripe on the blackthorn, to make his wife some sloe gin, he heard the startled 'chucks!' of a cock pheasant. The bird, splendid in its own autumn bronzes which rivalled the leaves on the trees, put up from almost beneath his feet to fly low toward the weir.

Too low as it happened. Shappy saw the bird, then Bramble bounding after it with not a sound. He watched transfixed as his dog caught up with the bird then drew alongside to leap and bring his quarry down. A furious flurry of wings ensued then all was still as the lurcher leaned upon his prey.

"Here boy", Shappy called quietly. The lurcher gathered his prize in powerful jaws, bringing it to Shappy and dropping it at his feet.

"Dearie me Bramble, and me retired from this game. I'm aveard us'll have to tell Jack. That's a thumpin gert bird boy, you'm a fine dog. Us had better way be getting homalong".

Shappy patted the lurcher's head and picking up the pheasant he turned away from the weir to retrace his steps homeward. Then Shappy froze, calling 'stay boy' to Bramble as the hairs on his neck tingled and an icy finger of dread touched along his spine.

Up ahead, glowing luminous against the westward darkening sky he could see a light bobbing about at what he estimated twenty feet in the air. He stood very still, knowing Bramble had also seen it for a low growl issued from the lurcher already excited by his recent kill. "Stay boy", Shappy repeated.

Shappy was not a man who feared much in life. Tough, with years of night poaching in often pitch darkness when the sound of badger or hedgehog rustling nearby could have the average person running for home, he was used to most things that went bump in the night. But this was not of that ilk. This was silent, bobbing gently over the field and glowing, of that he was absolutely sure. And it was coming towards him.

"Stay boy", he said again though there was no movement from Bramble whatsoever. His own feet would not move. Was it Jack with a lantern walking towards him? He giggled hysterically. Jack O Lantern, he thought. Funny that. But this luminous light, whatever it was rose even higher, higher than the hedgebank and no-one was carrying it. Then dipping, swaying and bobbing it came towards them again, growing larger, glowing more strongly.

Shappy gripped the pheasant, wishing he'd brought his blackthorn stick. I'll have to hit it with the pheasant if it comes any too close, he thought, then his heart leapt as a blood curdling screech came from the direction of the glowing phenomenon.

Another screech, then Shappy saw the creature now only some twenty paces from them, dipping low, was a barn owl. It was Mist, hunting the field from the elder tree. Shappy realised he'd been holding his breath and he exhaled and breathed in deeply, settling his nerves.

"You silly bugger, owl!" he called, then laughing he cried to both owl and dog, "What a dawbake I am!"

But Mist was glowing. She was not merely white in the darkness. Shappy could see her hazily glowing, ethereal, something he had never seen before in his life. He watched her turn to wing her way across the field once more in the direction of the dark woods for the daylight was now but a sliver of paleness on the far horizon, and he could still see her, smaller now but 'lit', and then she was gone amongst the trees.

Shappy wandered home slowly, still shaken by the strange encounter. When he described the incident to his wife, and later to the farmer, he said how for a moment or two he had thought of UFOs and alien beings, it was that eerie.

Jack who had also been told of the pheasant and told Shappy to eat it and enjoy it, admitted that in all his farming years he had never seen the like.

Several weeks later Shappy met up with the naturalist friend in the local Friday market place and was told that he had seen the same phenomenon only twice in 40 years of serious wildlife watching.

"I may be wrong", the naturalist told him, "but in my own mind I am quite sure it has to do with honey tuft fungi which is parasitic on trees and very common".

He went on to explain to Shappy that trees and their branches stricken with the fungi became luminous and glowed in the night. He himself used tree limbs so stricken, as edging to the pathways at his nature sanctuary, so as to move about more freely in the dark. He said that he had seen foxes coming along the pathways at night with glowing green 'socks', and the owl situation at least twice, the birds having perched and rubbed against the honey tuft fungi- affected trees during their hunting forays.

He said it is so excellent he even tested it as a glow worm lure and could see his own fingers glowing green in the dark when he had handled timber on which the honey tuft grew.

So it was that some of the ghost sights of nights spent in the countryside were explained, and the barn owls, ghostly enough in their own way, had had their dimmity glowing explained by someone who knew the countryside like the back of his hand.

Chapter 7

November end and one frosty morning when the whole valley sparkled white and jewel- like Mist awoke to a new sound thrusting itself into her ears with a harshness that caused fear in every fibre of her being. The night before she had eaten well, a brown rat caught in the farmyard nearby as it was burrowing into the hedge bank as part of a well used rat run in the area. Thus she had slept well in her ash tree hollow, snug and warm, for ivy curtained the old tree to half its height. Now rudely awakened the owl flicked her wings, rising to the perch above her main shelter, to gaze out across the silvery frosted landscape.

The sound, louder now and shaking the air, came from just along the wood edge some fifty human paces from Mist's ash tree. She saw two humans crouched beside an oak tree that had grown from an acorn 300 years before. The screaming sound came louder. Mist saw a fox break cover to run beneath her, the animal vanishing into the woods, as a grey squirrel dashed across her vision. Mist watched as the oak she had often perched upon suddenly leaned into the field and with its own creaking screams fall with a huge rending of large branches and falling soil and stones, its life ended by chain saws in less time than it had taken the acorn of its birth to take shoot 300 years before.

"Look, a barn owl!" One of the men shouted to his companion and they paused to watch the bird rise from the hollow ash to wing her way up, over the treetops and out of their vision.

"Not bad. A fox and now an owl", the man said. "This is a good job to have if you want to see wildlife".

"Can't hear a word you're saying". His workmate said.

"These ear muffs". And he moved away to begin chain sawing the branches away from the main trunk of the oak.

Mist, still hearing the terrible sounds of the screaming chainsaw, flew high over the treetops, heading for the other side of the woodlands away from the valley she knew so well. Below her, leafless trees showed black against the frosted land as a veil of mist rose towards the warming sun. She flew over fields of brown and green, finding the Yeo River beneath her, then woodlands known as Coxleigh and Sepscott. Here Mist faltered then leaving the river she flew north to Shirwell passing over the churchyard where, unknown to her, one of her brothers lived. He hunted the church area and Youlston Estate and was even now fast asleep in a barn close by the village of Shirwell. Mist flew on, holding northward over The Warren woodland, then over North Woolley and Woolley Woods to reach Arlington Court. Here she perched for a while on a tall, stone construction by a lake but a grey heron alight-ing nearby drove her on, over a road where once again she found the River Yeo. The winter sun warmed Mist's back and she felt its rays giving her strength though she was tired and unused to such long daytime flying.

Mist dipped lower, following the river beneath Parsonage Wood to suddenly come upon a cleave on a steep east facing valley side where a flock of redwings fed along a tall hedge. Across the cleave was another woodland with a freshwater marsh by the river. Mist flew across the steep slope seeing trees before her and an open cavity in the fork of one of these. She dipped one wing, swinging in a wide curve to alight easily onto the flat floor of the cavity and turning she began to preen and watch the valley.

Below her was an old badger sett and scattered about the wood, three small buildings timber built. No sound disturbed the day save for the calls of rooks and crows in a distant field and the patter of melting frost water striking the leaf litter below her vantage point. Mist turned, moving back against the rear of her new shelter and with one last glance to assure herself all was well she slept.

In the building nearest to where Mist slept, a wooden shed of no more than 6ft x 4ft, a man smiled happily to himself, patting his collie dog on the head. He could hardly believe he had actually seen a barn owl enter the nest box he and a friend had erected in the oak tree over two years before. Wood pigeons had nested in it the first spring and squirrels had used it but barn owls, no. To one day find them using it was a likelihood but to see a barn owl fly up over his land, take to the box and remain in it was a dream come true, he thought. He made brief notes on a writing pad and happily locked the shed door, his 'office' door, his Sanctuary, a sanctuary for all wildlife who wished to stay.

"Let's go home old son", he called to his dog.

Midnight, the valley dark with shadows as Mist awoke with a start from her deep sleep of recovery after the flight of some six or seven miles as an owl flies. She moved to the edge of her new found roost, gazing down at the sounds that had awoken her. Large shapes like the cattle she knew in the Yeo Valley moved gently below her through the trees. They were red deer hinds, eight of them, with two calves of the year born in the previous June. Lower in the woodland a stag watched the open hillside, quiet and peaceful now, like the land, for the rut of the red deer had ended in October and he was at peace with the world.

Mist watched them move out onto the cleave which was the steep open field between two woods, once part of the greater wood before trees were felled to provide more grazing land.

Sounds of human voices and music came on the wind from far away, but the animals of the wild woods paid it no heed. The sounds came from the inn some half a mile distant along the road above the valley for it was Christmas Eve and people without children to look after at home were celebrating the Christian festival with food, drink and revelry.

Mist, who did not know of such things, flew out from her perch to drop upon other sounds, finding a plump vole in her talons. She swallowed the vole standing on a fallen tree which gave her views down to the marsh and silver ribbon of river, and beyond over the fields and spinneys of well kept farmland.

Despite the night she could see well and her hearing was so acute she caught three more voles, eating them all to assuage her hunger, to warm her for leaner times should they come about.

Mist felt safe here, in the way wild creatures feel safe. A mixture of peace and contentment rarely considered by humans. Natural. Food, shelter, that is all wild creatures need basically, and the love of a mate in the case of some species.

Deep in the woods a tawny owl called and Mist could hear another replying in the distance. 'kee-wick, tu-whooo'. Then a dog fox barked its high pitched call three times and Mist settled back to listen to the night sounds of Christmas-time.

Chapter 8

It had rained for most of seven days. Mist had hunted between the rainy spells which were not showers but prolonged bouts of solid wetness. Rivulets of water ran from the pooling up of rain behind the earth hedge bank at the top of the woods, leaving streams of soil in wavy patterns down over the wood slope amongst the trees. But undeterred, the first chiff chaffs for the year had arrived, the springtime vanguard of incoming migrant species from the African continent, to feed up on what insects they could find, many days before the first swallows.

The oaks were leafing well, 'the oak before the ash', a local farmer had chuckled to his wife for they knew this was usually the way of it these days, the old weather adage no longer the prophetic sign it was a decade or two ago.

And on the eighth day the skies cleared. There was no belt of cloud to follow that which now drifted over Exmoor, spending the last of its rain upon the sodden farmland. Suddenly there was sunshine, the woodland pattering with raindrops falling from leafing branches already soaking up the warmth, drying in its gentle caress. Primroses and dog violets lit the hedgebank within the woods as celandines and wood anemones reached for the sunshine and opened wide to reveal their gold and white flowers. A chiff chaff began singing from its hazel perch beside the gate into the cleave, its tiny feathered body bursting with the pleasure of having found the very nest hollow he and his mate had raised five young in during the previous year. As he sang his 'chiff-chaff' notes a blue tit flitted by him to alight on a wooden nestbox affixed to an oak, the little bird bristling with spring time fervour as she inspected the box entrance then went inside to consider her sudden choice of a home for her future young more carefully, eating the spiders eggs about the edge of the box as she did so.

In the ancient badger sett half way down the wood slope a two year old sow badger lay on her side suckling her two cubs born on the first day of the month of March. The cubs were four weeks old, the only cubs born to this sett for two years and now its nine occupants lay sleeping save for herself though she half dozed as her two young ones fed from the goodness issuing from her warming body.

Further into the woods along and just below a well worn deer path a vixen lay with her four cubs of the year, born shortly after the badger cubs. She was named Shadow by the landowner who would sometimes call her on autumn and winter days when she would trot to him by his hut to take half a pasty. She had learned to trust him when he tossed such a morsel to her as she chanced upon him along the hut path two years before. She had been hungry, the aroma of the warm pasty too tempting. Now there was a bond between them though she kept him to herself and did not visit with cubs, nor did he call her at such times. Shadow would feed the cubs with her milk for five weeks and begin to regurgitate food at about that time, the cubs being fully weaned at six weeks old, certainly by seven weeks and before the waxing and waning of two moons.

At times Shade, her mate, had brought food for her and now on this day of warming sunshine she would leave the earth and cubs to lie up close by, to watch the woodlands as is the way of foxes. Her mate often lay up beneath the timber built hide, raised about a foot from the ground on poles. Here the landowner had stored timber and formed a cavern. Safe and dry from bad weather, the dog fox spent much of his time here at a ready made earth, watching down to the earth Shadow his mate had dug long before.

By mid May the cubs would be about the earth, playing amongst the trees and gradually learning to hunt for themselves on evening forays with the vixen, oft times accompanied by her mate, for the cubs would move on come the autumn, to find territories of their own.

The farmland all about was hunted by the local Fox Hound pack, The Dulverton West, but the landowner had agreed a 'ban' on hunting on his land, managing it as a private Nature Reserve where wildlife came first, people second. The Hunt strictly honoured the ban, sending a copy each year of their hunt programme for the district in order that the owner could monitor and observe if he wished to see they kept away.

But now it was the time of primroses and violets, the woodland floor beneath Mist's home a carpet of palest yellow with greens and violets showing through. Wood anemones too, the wind flowers, whitely shone, opening to the warming sunshine, almost hurrying to bloom before the tree leaf canopy veiled the woodland floor with its shade, to remove the light which opened the flowers each day.

A bright yellow brimstone butterfly, yellower than the primroses, felt the sun's warmth on his wing. Stirring from his ivy lair where he had spent the winter in hibernation he flew out along the woodland path, seeking a female, passing the hut where the landowner worked swiftly at waterproofing the timber for another year.

He grinned as he saw the first brimstone of the year flutter by, making a mental note to write the sighting into his diary in the hut. Almost finished at the task of protecting his "hut' timbers he sniffed appreciatively at the delicious aroma of sausages and bacon cooking away on a camping stove nearby. His favourite time of year was beginning, the rebirth of the natural year with six months of spring and summer ahead.

A chiff chaff called and robin song had turned from winter silver to summer gold. Various tits were at nestboxes all about the woods and he knew by May month the brimstones would have eggs. He had planted many alder buckthorn whips in the woods and adjoining field, adding to that which already grew on site for it was the food plant of the butterfly and vital to their future.

He stroked his paint brush along the bottom timber of the hut and with a sigh of satisfaction stood back to survey his handiwork, then strolled to whence his breakfast sizzled, cooked and ready to be enjoyed with a bread roll, butter and coffee. No white table linen, sparkling cutlery and crockery, just rustic fare on his corduroy clad knees, sitting on an old plank seat by the hut side. He would leave a sausage for the vixen to take at her leisure, and remembering she had cubs to feed he grinned, putting two aside for her, sure that she would smell the aroma of cooking wafting amongst the trees.

Another brimstone flew by, springtime was stirring and he wondered how Mist the barn owl was faring in the nest box he had put up some years before. As it was, Mist was perched half dozing, at the edge of her home, eyes closed but ears tuned to every sound. She could differentiate between the rustling of tree leaves and branches and the sounds made by active mammals, hearing as much as seeing making her and her kind the successful hunters they are.

Mist knew there was a human working in the woods but he was often about and did not bother her. Sometimes she would see him and one or two others down by the river with a dog, quite clearly from her vantage point. Now she could hear movement along the deer path beneath her. Staring down she could see no deer or large animal, only slight movement amongst the grasses to one side and she was hungry.

Though she could not see the creature below she knew roughly of its size, locating her prey by ear rather than by eye. Mist flew out and down, pouncing on a rat that had been crossing the field from the nearby farm, raising her wings as she made impact then lowering them to regain her balance as the rat died in her fearsome talons. She opened her eyes wide now, having half closed them to protect them from the tall, stiff vegetation about her, then rising on powerful, silent wings she returned with the dead rat to her nestbox home.

Sausages and bacon, or dead rat. To each his own. Mist gazed sleepily down across the steep cleave to the marshes and river. Her food for the day freshly acquired she rested before eating as the first swallows began to arrive along the valley, taking insects as they swooped and soared above the Yeo River. Silver light on the water, the meandering, shining river winding through pale lit meadows and beneath the two woods on the hillside. The line of water, broken twice only by old stone bridges was clearly seen by Mist as she flew high to alight on the stark, gnarled branches of an oak tree which had die-back in its ancient crown. Mist's perch was the daytime vantage point of a buzzard who lived in the largest of the two woodlands with his mate of three years, the hawks now fast asleep amongst the shadowy trees.

Mist watched the wide 'V' wake of an otter approaching upstream below her. She saw the animal leave the water to shiver drops of moonlight, spraying the grasses and sedges until they too, shone with a myriad fairy jewels beneath the full moon. The otter dropped a rainbow trout upon the river bank and began to eat, the sounds of sharp teeth on raw fish carrying clearly to the owls ears, its coat as spiked as its teeth as it dried in the moonlight.

The rainbow trout was one of several that had strayed from a fish farm downstream of the village, trout which now lived and bred the length of the waterway when once only the native brown trout made its home here along with smaller fish species, until humans had begun the farming of fish two decades before. But Mist was not a fish eater though she had seen tawny owls catch fish from the shallows of a weir pool near her old home.

Mist was hungry in the way of owls who ate well, living in countryside where food was not scarce save for the harshest times of winter. But needing food she launched from the ancient oak, silent, but causing the otter eating trout below to look upwards to her ghostly white form, for he had seen her shadow leave the shadow of the oak tree on the river bank before him.

Out across the wild freshwater marsh field Mist flew on rapid wing beats, quartering the ground swiftly and low, ears listening for sounds in the high grasses and other vegetation. High pitched squeaking below her and Mist dropped, her weight holding a common shrew which she ate, but still hungry she flew on below the wood bottom.

Reaching the open fields beyond the wood Mist flew following the upward slope of trees, coming to the roadway. She perched on a gatepost, hearing the loud noise of vehicles and she waited. Weeks ago she had flown along this road at night to find herself blinded by vehicle lights and buffeted by the sudden winds caused by its passing, to find herself on her back upon the platform-like top of a flailed hedge. Mist had recovered to pull herself upright, her eyes seeing only flashing lights as two other vehicles swept by to enter the inn car park further along the road. But she had learned to avoid them now, her memory storing the fear she had felt from this noisy creature of the roads.

Even now as two cars passed swiftly by her she felt their wind blow, gripping the gatepost with clenching talons to prevent being blown from her perch, closing eyes to the blinding lights and the dust swirl as the great beasts roared by and were gone into the darkness of the night.

Mist flew from her perch, crossing the road and over the hedge, following a double row of trees which hid the narrow path to the village church and churchyard. Gravestones stood stark in the darkness, some as white as the owl herself. Perched upon one of these Mist appeared as a carved owl image, part of the cold stone, then she pounced, catching in one swift movement one of several wood mice which lived about the church, though it offered them little sanctuary from owls or other predators of the night.

Mist ate and rested then caught and ate another wood mouse before flying high above the churchyard then recognising familiar fields and woods she crossed the road at treetop height to wing her way homewards. Here she perched on a branch beside her nest box home, dozing, digesting her kills and watching the night-time valley.

Chapter 9

The day had dawned cloudy to the point of darkness, the east facing hillside swept with a fine drizzle from off nearby Exmoor. In the woods behind Mist's southerly facing home pied flycatchers and redstarts were nesting in boxes along with several resident species. From her vantage point Mist had watched nuthatches taking flakes of bark, leaves and moss into the nest box fixed to an oak tree near her and now on the first day of May the female had laid her first egg, the male nuthatch always about. He would sometimes whistle with rapid flute-like notes or call 'tvett, tvett, tvett' to let his mate know he was nearby.

Blue, great and coal tits were already incubating eggs in some of the many nest boxes about the ancient woodland and soon, too, the summer visiting flycatchers and redstarts would lay, and raise young.

Mist dozed. She had eaten well on voles and had caught a mole that night in the field between the woods and the road so was content and dry in her home. Seven red deer hinds stood quietly together in the wood bottom sheltered from the rain by trees and a high bank with a hedgerow upon it. Further in where the wood was densest a stag stood at peace but forlorn looking, his head sore from recently shed antlers which now lay within feet of each other on the riverbank below the woods.

"May Day". Mist did not hear the voice of the landowner as he unlocked the gate at the top of the woods. "Must come out on May Day, rain or shine", he said to the collie dog at his heels. He led the dog through the wet mist of bluebells carpeting much of the woods. A glimmer of sunshine sent pale beams to seek out the blur as the rain ceased, leaving the land refreshed and soaking.

As he neared his small hut the landowner noted several of his nest boxes were occupied, various tits flying about, some perching on the roofs, some flitting inside. He grinned cheerfully as he saw a male pied flycatcher, splendidly black and white, calling from beside a nest box in an oak. 'First for the year' he thought as he opened up the hut and went in, followed by his dog. He dusted around the tiny hut then picking up his binocular he strolled along a pathway he had cut with a spade several years before, which led to a timber hide and an old plank seat. Reaching the hide he looked inside just as a male blackbird began its alarm calls close by. Then he saw why. On a shelf he had built into the hide wall as a place to rest elbows to better view the woodland was a nest with a female blackbird sitting, gleaming dark eyes watching him.

"Doesn't look as if we'll be using the hide for a few days after all Willow", he said to the collie who had seen the bird on its nest and was whining softly.

"We'd better way move on Willow". The man clicked his fingers, walking away along the path followed by the dog. The two made their way to where the plank seat stood moss covered from lack of use, the man sitting down on the green velvet moss cushion to watch the woods, From his vantage point he could see a dozen of the many nest boxes he had erected and numbered. He began to watch these, making notes on a pad as he saw birds at them.

Time passed swiftly, man and dog enjoying the spring woodlands in their differing ways. For a while Willow had sniffed about along the pathway, excited by the many scents. Once a wood mouse had run from his questing nose, the dog watching with his black 'butterfly' ears pricked forward as the tiny animal disappeared amongst bluebells. Later a weasel followed along the scent trail of the wood mouse, to lose it amongst the wetness of the earlier rain.

When the sun reached high above the bottom corner of the woods nearest the river the man rose stiffly and calling the dog who was now laid dozing by his side, he moved back along the path toward the hut.

"Time for sandwiches old son", he said quietly and grinned as the dog moved swiftly by him to be waiting alert for food when he arrived at the hut. Sitting on his wooden folding chair he pulled a bag from an old forces haversack which also held a flask of tea.

"May Day treat Willow", he chuckled, "look a steak and kidney pie for each of us, and cheddar sandwiches. Now what's better than that and bluebells by the door?"

The two ate hungrily, the collie then stretching out on the grass beside the hut door where sunlight had warmed and dried his favourite spot.

From the hut more nest boxes could be seen and for a while the man wrote busily on his note pad all that he could see at each box. Later in the month he would have a quick look inside the boxes to seek details of progress, then leave the birds to their own devices. He saw the nest boxes he had provided as a sort of compensation gesture to the wild users of the many natural tree holes lost to heavy woodland felling in the area over recent years. It was part of his philosophy to return, or give back, as much as he could for all the joy and pleasure the countryside had given him through his life. Thus he had planted trees and encouraged wild plants that were the food plants of butterflies and moths, and generally managed his land holding as a nature reserve, ever seeking to make gains and provide benefits for the native flora and fauna.

"Wonder how Mist is getting along Willow?" he said to his dog who raised his head, gazing with gentle brown eyes into his owners face then laid it back again on sun warmed turf with a great sigh.

Focusing his binocular he shifted himself so as to gaze down over the woodland to where he could just see a part of one side of the owl box which was largely obscured from his sight by fresh green oak leaves and branches. There was a warbler, a chiff chaff he thought, and a wood pigeon on a nest. A good find that, he thought, and made further notes on his pad.

Within the box Mist dozed, hearing the slumberous, deep cooing of the pigeon who was sitting on two newly laid eggs, his mate sunning on a branch close by him. The chiff chaff ate insects from the leaves about him then called 'chiff chaff, chiff chaff', to his mate in a nest built by her in a tangle of herbs against a buckthorn shrub. She had laid the first two of her, usually, five eggs, white like those of the pigeon but with spotted purple-brown markings. She had nested and raised young here the previous year as is the way of chiff chaffs and willow warblers.

In the village of scattered houses straggling over the distant hillside a postman looked skywards as he left his red vehicle to deliver a parcel, seeing the arrival of a dozen swifts as they flew by above him.

That'll be the church swifts, he thought. Back again, that'll please the vicar. He knew that each year the swifts returned to the floor of the church tower. The old building, beautifully situated on land held by the National Trust, had a lake and pond adjoining, with many trees and shrubs about. He recalled his boyhood days in the village, of going to the now disused school and how jackdaws and barn owls had nested in the church tower at various times over the years.

"Swifts be back again Fred". The postman pointed upwards as

he handed the parcel to Fred Pickard, a retired farm worker born in the next village seven decades before.

"Aye boy. Followed een the swallows and martins. They'm already nesting and I saw a barn owl up by the church last Sunday night when I took the dug out Brian. Bin a while since I saw one up there boy I can tell ee".

"Strewth yes. Takes me back that does. I was only thinking just now how they and the jackdaws was always about the church til a few years ago".

The two men chatted briefly of blackbirds and fishing and of changing times then parted, promising a pint in the local come the weekend.

Black as night against the sky the swifts hawked insects in screaming flight, hurling themselves in the air about the church tower in a frenzy of joy at reaching the end of their journey from the African continent.

'Sreeee-sreee-sreee', they called, feeding on the wing, feeding up for in a day or two they would be catching wind blown straw and feathers in mid-air to build their scant, rudimentary nests in holes about the church tower.

Within the tower, perched upon a pile of old ropes roughly coiled in one corner away from an opening carved in stone, a male barn owl half dozed, half listened to the new sounds of screaming swifts. He saw their black shapes pass and repass at speed and he grew restless as spring sunshine warmed his roost. A wasp buzzed about him then flew out into the day and he wanted to follow but the brightness of the morning held him where he perched.

The owl had three roosting sites in the area, the others being a barn stacked high with old beer barrels made of wood and hooped with iron, and an old tiled round house on a farm across the river valley which was once the village pound for local miscreants needing to cool off from a night of too much ale, or caught poaching. Over the years the cob and tiled building, which only held one person, had fallen into disrepair but had now been lovingly restored by the landowner, complete with an open window slit.

The owl stared as the banging of the church door echoed into the tower but he dozed again for it was a sound he had often heard once or twice during a day. Below him beyond his vision a woman put fresh water in a vase, placing a huge bunch of spring flowers near the carved wooden pulpit for the morrows services. It was Saturday and soon people would be arriving at the big house, visitors of the National Trust for its property was open to the public from Easter to October in every year.

She sighed, then hummed contentedly to herself, hearing the swifts and seeing them and several swallows beyond the window of stained glass, as coloured shadows zooming by. The sound of a motor mower came loud and she smiled knowing her husband had begun to mow the lawns around the old building. Between them they kept the land about the church, and the flowers within and without in good order, as her parents had done before her.

For much of the day the noise of the motor mower and the occasional banging of doors kept the owl from full sleep. More people were entering and leaving, looking about then signing the visitor's book with their names and places or origin. Then a coach load of people invaded, led by a local guide itching to get them all down to the lake to see the heronry with its fifty or sixty great grey birds nesting in the treetops.

Bang! Bang! Loud voices, footsteps on gravel. Then all was silent. The owls roosting lair became an orange pink glow as the sunset told of a fine day on the morrow. Eight pipistrelle bats flew into the dusk followed by the owl whose thoughts were on a quieter roost, and food.....

Chapter 10

Mist awoke with a start, hearing the bark of a dog close by and a human voice. The dog became silent, obeying his owner's request to be quiet and Mist saw the two sitting above the badger sett at the wood edge below her own home. Unseen and silent she launched from the owl nesting box that was her home to fly across Brock Cleave to Parsonage Wood where she followed the trees down over the cleave, then over the marsh to the river and beyond.

It was at the crossing of the river that Mist was seen by the landowner who, badger watching with his dog, was delighted to know she was still about and using the nest box at the wood edge. Excited by the sight of a barn owl he watched Mist wing her pale and silent way over his marsh field, over the Yeo River, to the small fields beyond that he often explored to take photographs of the unusual white flowered marsh thistles that grew there each summer. He turned on his red-filtered spotlight to see the owl become pink in its warm glow, then she was gone amongst the trees.

Mist flew on to perch on an oak branch over a small stone

bridge where the river rushed white beneath its single arch then slowed to wind its way as a trout stream to the Taw, and thence to the sea. Below the owl a dipper slept in a nest built into the bridge arch, five eggs warm beneath her body. The dipper, a diurnal bird, would incubate the eggs for 16 days, fed by her mate until their young hatched to become part of the waterway life in the valley.

Mist watched the river and fields but she still did not feel hunger. A badger moved along the riverbank, crossing the bridge to the pasture fields where it began to dig for earthworms.

A half moon lit the valley, rain cloud shadows moving slowly across the hillside as a small herd of red deer hinds followed the hedge to patter through an open gateway into a field with cattle, where they began to graze.

From far off Mist heard the hissing scream of another barn owl in flight. 'Shreee-shreee', the calls came again, louder, nearer. To the badger watcher with his dog the sounds could be likened to a soul in torment, but he grinned, knowing the call for what it was, the contact call of one owl to another.

To Mist, still upon her perch, the calls told of another of her kind in the area she regarded as her own. She bristled, moving from one foot to the other as she gazed and listened in the direction from which the sounds came.

'Shreee'. From closer now, the call drew her eyes to an old green lane that began at a farm road and petered out half way across a large meadow. Once there was a hedge here and a wide gateway leading into smaller fields but the farmer had grubbed up the hedges to form one large field 'to gain more grass' as he put it.

And then Mist saw the other barn owl. It appeared suddenly, white and floating above the hazel and hawthorn along the green lane, in slow flight with flapping wings and short glides. She watched the owl fly lower then follow the river bank towards her, to drop and make a kill, then rise again to a fence post holding barbed wire in place.

Mist launched from her perch with a loud screech. Flying swift and direct towards the new owl in her territory, she perched abruptly on the fence post next to the one on which the interloper hunched watching her. For long moments the two perched, staring tensely until the Arlington Church owl, for it was he, left his perch to drop his recently caught field vole on the grass before Mist's post.

Mist trembled as the male owl flew above and about her. She uttered husky, throaty, hiss-like calls stretching high on her perch in begging ritual, unlearned yet known instinctively by all barn owls. Then, screeching again Mist flew with rapid wing beats across the meadow pursued by the male. They flew thus in a frenzy of dashing flight, Mist twisting and turning in her excitement, the male matching her every move as they uttered alternate screeches in a frenzy of joy.

On the hillside hidden by tree shadows the landowner had forsaken badger-watching and with his dog was watching the two owls in their courtship ritual.

He saw Mist suddenly break her rapid circling and twisting to fly directly up onto a moonlit Scots pine branch, a lone tree by his own gateway into the adjoining paddock field. Here she perched as the male hung almost kestrel-like in the air before her, his fluttering display flight keeping his staring eyes on a level with Mist's.

Again Mist flew this time in slow flight, pale and majestic screeching again to have the male owl chase her out of sight at the wood bottom. Here the male left her to fly into the old linhay which backed onto the stone wall of the nature sanctuary. Mist followed him into the open fronted building, finding him perched on the loft platform which formed a flat timber ceiling to half the linhay.

Mist flew out again into the moonlight, screeching in unison with the male, who followed her, chased her about the marsh field beneath her nest box home where she perched atop it, fluttering and trembling at him with slightly open wings. The male flew behind her and screeching loudly she took him as her mate.

Later the male flew down, catching another vole which he brought to his mate, tearing and feeding her with the fresh meat.

"I think we'd best be gone and leave 'em to it", the landowner said quietly to his dog and they clambered up over the steep hillside to the road and their waiting car.

Trevor Beer's FIVE OWLS

2

Athene - The Little Owl

Prologue

A pair of little owls had lived all winter in the old orchard at Mill Farm, a 'small farm' in Devon, worked organically and hidden away along a tree lined lane.

The winter has been a kind one, one of a succession of mild if sometimes wet and windy winters when seasons seem to merge rather than be clearly defined by changing weather conditions as in the recent past.

The female little owl first saw the light of day in an old mine adit some four miles from Mill Farm towards the coast. She was one of four young hatched about one human pace within the grey, forbidding looking mine entrance, in a man-made crevice of quarry stone hidden by a curtain of ivy and bramble which trailed down over the ever open entrance. Only twice had the owls seen humans when local geology groups arrived to explore the old mine workings, to take samples from the spoil heaps just without the stone walls. Deeper within the mine was a roost of lesser horseshoe bats, unnoticed by the geology group and known only to one or two local naturalists.

The little owls and bats co-existed without conflict of any kind. The mine was a perfect shelter for both species. In winter the bats hung close to the ground in spaces in the adit wall about

18ins apart just beyond a deep pool of water close to the entrance which deterred most human prowlers. In summer the bat roost was used as a nursery colony by pregnant females, the adult males moving out to a huge cedar tree standing amidst much holly and hazel.

Athene's mother had discovered her own nest site near the adit entrance when fleeing a storm that had chased her to shelter during the first week of her dispersal as an independent owl, one of two nestlings of an ageing mother. She had found the long disused mine shaft to her liking, and food in abundance so she had stayed, mated and remained. Athene was of her first brood and she and her mate had worked hard to rear all four young during what had been a dry summer with very little disturbance.

Athene had been the first of the brood to fly free. Circling the mine shaft areas several times she had finally swooped by her parents to follow a river valley, then many hedgerows and a lane leading off a minor road until she had flown exhausted into the Mill Farm orchard.

Chapter 1

With a flutter of grey-brown wings flecked with white, Athene the female little owl left her tree-hole in the ancient hedgerow and the house mouse below her died, crushed by her small black powerful talons. Athene stood by the entrance to a rabbit burrow below her nest site, swallowing the tiny mouse whole, then she flew up to perch on a tree branch, standing quietly to look down over the steep meadow adjoining her orchard home.

Beside her, three white eggs lay in the tree hole on debris that time alone had allowed to fall, for Athene, like other little owls, was no nest builder. She looked about her, seeing her mate on a fence post some fifty feet away where primroses scented the moist spring-time air with their delicate perfume.

The primroses grew in pale yellow cushions along the hedge bank and out into the field which was empty of livestock and growing hay. Violets showed here and there amongst the primroses and the first bluebells of the year thrust skywards.

The hedgerow was one of three boundary hedges about a triangular old orchard, Athene's home an ancient hawthorn gnarled and twisted from a century of growth. Twenty years before, a bullace tree had fallen to a storm when part of the hedge bank collapsed, the old plum tearing at its own roots, tearing at the hawthorn in its falling, but both trees had survived. Both bore the fruits each year of their own kind, the 'crystals' of the bullace even now collected by the farming landowner on occasions for the making of home-made wine, the haws or aglets of the hawthorn left as a feast for wintering birds.

The hawthorn, which the farmer's wife always called May, had been rent asunder by the falling of the bullace but had withstood the crushing weight, opening only to widen the fork holding the old plum tree, then holding her own place. Thus the two trees had come together, living quietly linked for two decades during which time the hole in the hawthorn had formed a timber cavern sheltered by its own foliage and that of the bullace tree.

Athene with a last glance at her mate flew up and into the nest hole to continue the third week of incubation of her three eggs. She called 'Kiew', to her mate who replied using the same call before he flew up onto the roof of a red brick building of the local Water Authority built on the farmer's land and screened by newly planted hawthorns and blackthorns, growing outside a wire fence. From here Athene's mate could watch over her and their territory by day for little owls are diurnal in the main, birds of the day, active in hunting mainly at dusk and dawn.

In the orchard overlooked by the little owl nest the first cuckoo flowers, or milkmaids, of the year were in pale pink bloom. Lady's Smock they were also called, the favourite flower of the adders who lived in the nearby hedgerows and basked in the old orchard when the sun was hot. Country folk told their children 'never to pick milkmaids or you'll be bitten by an adder afore the year is out m'dears'.

And so the old belief had passed down through the Brown family who had farmed the land for four generations, to Alice Mary Brown who sat in the meadow on sunshiney days to watch the wildlife. She was now ten years of age. Alice received her education via home tutoring. She had been quite ill following a bout of bullying at her school on the edge of a nearby town, thus her parents had decided to deal with her education themselves. In her second year of home tutoring Alice was well ahead with her subjects, her work pleasing the inspector who called once a year to 'check up'.

She quickly regained her health, the bullying and stress removed from her young life, her parents finding her love for nature the everlasting tonic she needed and which now so enriched hers and their own lives.

Alice received the same holidays as did the schools in the area, this helping the Browns to remember the vacation periods though they often added a day on at each end as Alice was so far ahead with most of her lessons and very bright.

Alice knew all about the birds nesting in 'her' orchard. Her father had told her the orchard was hers for as long as he did not need the land for anything else on the farm and the building of a tree house confirmed in Alice's mind that the orchard belonged to her and all the wild creatures and plants that lived within and around it.

No-one came to the orchard much, other than to shout 'tea!' or 'dinner time!' to Alice, from over the hedge, so the triangle of land was very much hers, to love and know. She did not know that the binocular hanging on a hook in the Brown's kitchen was used regularly by her parents to ensure all was well in the orchard. She had her own small binocular, which she called 'knocklers', in her tree house. She knew how to use her eyes, missing very little that went on in the orchard.

Now Alice was on Easter holidays, three weeks of fun in the

orchard, which she loved dearly, then it would be the long summer holiday. Athene, hidden in her tree hole on her eggs, heard the sound of her mate's call 'kiew' coming twice to her ears. She crouched low, then hearing footfalls passing the tree and receding in the distance she bobbed her head up to focus on the cause. A human. And one she knew well as often about the orchard. She bobbed down then up again, seeing her mate doing likewise on his roof top perch. 'Kiew'. Her mate called again, softly, and she knew there was no threat to her or her eggs.

Athene's mate, who had been hatched from one of four eggs in a rabbit burrow three miles away, watched the human climb the four steps to the tree house, to go inside. He had roosted inside with Athene on stormy nights and they had caught moths from its roof, and lizards, dropping on the prey from ambush.

Again he bobbed up and down, seeing the human appear at the open window, then he crouched to become very still as he watched.

Alice looked about her, scanning the orchard through her binocular, feeling nicely important in her tree house, with her own shelf with its notebook and pencil. She liked to write the date then make notes of what she saw and knew. Three books lay on a cushion on the floor, a bird field guide, a flower field guide and a copy of "The Wind In The Willows" by Kenneth Grahame. Already she had seen a real Mr.Badger, and Mole, Toad and Stoats and Weasels. She felt as if she knew the characters personally. It was her ambition to see Ratty in real life, a real live water vole but she knew she'd have to be down by the river or the old mill leat to see him and she was not allowed down there on her own.

"Hmmm", Alice murmured, "a bird on the roof again. I wonder if it is a starling?" No, she thought as she focussed her binocular carefully, it is a bit like a cat. Alice giggled. A feathery cat. Then her mind cleared as if a cloud lifted to let the sunshine in. "It's an owl", she said to herself, a small owl, quite a little owl.

Alice reached down for her bird book and as she rose again to look from the window she was just in time to see the bird launch from the rooftop perch to fly swiftly to a tree in the hedge near her orchard gate. The bird flew in a bouncy fashion, up and down as if riding on waves, then perching it stared at her and began bobbing up and down.

How odd, Alice thought. What a nice, funny thing to do. A bouncy owl. She found 'Owl' in the book's index after a while and there beneath 'Barn, Eagle and Great Grey Owl' was 'Little', just as she had thought, quite a little owl.

Alice turned to the page the index told her to and there staring out of the page was her bird, with a frown on its face. She looked at the bird again through her binocular and sure enough it was one and the same with the picture. She read that the Little Owl was to be seen by day, so everything was just right. What a story to tell her parents in secret, she thought, then, oops, notebook. Taking up her pencil Alice wrote:

'I have a Little Owl in the orchard. It bobs up and down and watches me with yellow eyes'.

Excited she watched the owl a while longer she then began

listing other birds she knew well.

A male blackbird sang from the gate top where she came in to the orchard and in one apple tree a female chaffinch was building with grass. A nest! Alice wrote hurriedly. *'And there is our goldfinch at the end of the triangle'*. Alice knew goldfinches always nested in her orchard.

A robin sang sweetly from the pear tree nearby. She could not remember the name of the pear though her mother told her each year. And there's the two dunnocks shaking their wings again. She had had to tell her father they were not hedge sparrows, but that they were dunnocks. He had laughed and told her of the old names and how crackeys were wrens and blue tits were tom tits when he was a boy.

She could see blue tits now, looking in one of her three nest boxes. The boxes were numbered so she wrote *'blue tits at No2'* in her notebook. This was going to be a lovely Easter, she thought. Oh, and there is a treecreeper. Alice loved treecreepers and nuthatches for they came to the winter bird table placed outside the farm dining room windows, to eat peanuts and seed and things.

Overhead rooks swooped down towards the big rookery near the farm road. Back in the winter when the leaves were off the trees Alice had counted 37 nests. She had found a tree with what looked like lots of nests but her mother had explained they were witches brooms, made by insect attack on the tree.

Alice noted wood pigeon and then shouted aloud as what she was sure was a swallow zoomed by. *'Our swallows are back again'* she wrote, confident that others would soon be in to nest in the barn like every summer. *'It's spring today'*, she wrote and feeling hungry clambered down from the tree house to tell her parents of her little owls.

Chapter 2
Of Eggs and Young

Two days of rain followed, heavy April showers interspersed by periods of bright sunshine as more bluebells bloomed and the last of the lesser celandines gradually gave way to the later spring flowers.

Athene remained snug in her tree hole cavity, the fresh leaves of hawthorn and bullace adding to the already adequate shelter of the nest site. Her mate remained always close by but Athene came off the nest either early in the morning, or in the evenings to feed, depending how heavily it rained, usually taking small rodents but eating insects rather than go hungry.

Alice had taken her parents to see the male owl which had flown to the trees away from his mate's nest, calling cat-like as he did so.

"Brilliant Alice", her father had said, confirming the bird was a Little Owl. Leaning up on the second rung of the tree house ladder to look inside, his weight had suddenly snapped the rung and he noticed the drip of rain at the leaking roof. He promised Alice to sort it out quickly and winking at his wife they had swished home through the soaking grass, to tea.

Thus it was that Athene's nest site remained hidden from human eyes for up to that moment no-one had observed her leave the nest to feed. On the 25th day of Athene's incubation of her three eggs the sun rose warm in a clear sky, the dawn chorus including chiff chaff and willow warbler song and the calls of cock pheasants about the farm. It was Easter Friday, Good Friday, and in the hawthorn tree nest hollow lay three white, downy nestling little owls.

Chapter 3
Of Alice's New Hide

'Kiew'… Athene's mate, hunting for food for the three nestlings, called to her from the Bramley apple tree as the rumble of a vehicle sounded along the farm lane running by the orchard.

Two men alighted and working swiftly, brought large panels of timber into the orchard through the gateway, carrying them to where the tree house perched. Another vehicle arrived and the farmer joined the two men, chatting, working quietly, the little owls continuing to feed their young undisturbed.
"That's what it's all about chaps", grinned Jake Brown, "Our daughter is mad on wildlife, so this'll be her Easter and birthday present combined seeing she was born end of April".

"This will do her fine Jake. Would have loved this when I was a lad. And it'll last a few years". The older of the two workmen paused as his colleague pulled the green felted roof up into place and began to power screw it onto the four walls they had already positioned.

"Look at that, door and window looking right down across the orchard and the small window looking into the hedge at the back. Once we put these two shelves up the maid wont ever want to come home."

"Or go anywhere else either", called his colleague, finishing off the roofing. "There, that's done. Just glaze the windows and us'll be away. Where's Alice anyway?"

"Oh, she's reluctantly gone shopping with her mum. But hot cross buns and an Easter egg got her on the move early. She doesn't know about this of course".

"Ansome Jake. A real treat. And she's a fine maid you've got there".

"Yes. Likes to do her own thing natural history wise but good at lessons and helps her mum and me round the farm".

"Well you can't ask more'n that Jake. Cor I'd love to see her face when she sees this little lot. A snug little 6 foot by 4foot, dry and light, ansome stuff. Right then. Tis finished so us'll get out of the way. Let us know how it all goes."

The two men packed up their tools and drove off chuckling as Jake Brown drove his Land Rover back down to the farm after padlocking the new shed door.

An hour later Alice and her mother arrived home, Mrs Brown busying herself with making a pot of tea and warming hot cross buns. She was humming happily, having seen the new shed in the distance and receiving a wave from her husband.

"Will you need me much today mum?" Alice asked her mother.

"Well dear, I suppose not but I think your father has something he wants you to do. Here he comes now for a cuppa".

She put buns on plates, and mugs of tea as her husband washed his hands.

"Dad. What do you want me for, today? Will it take long?"

Jacob Brown grinned. "No Alice. Just want you to make sure the orchard is alright. I haven't mended that ladder of yours yet".

"Oh, well I'll miss that rung. I would like to write my note book every day". Alice ate hungrily from her hot cross bun. "These are nice, so's the tea. Yummy".

Jacob looked at his wife. "Well Mary. I think we'd best ways walk over with Alice, then go down and see how the cows are in bottom field."

"Right dear". She picked up the key ring with its new keys from the table. "Oh, Alice. Take these on ahead dear and if you see a padlock, open it up for us will you dear".

"If I see a padlock? What padlock Mum? Have we got a new lock somewhere?" She gazed mystified at her parents.

"Well yes. In a way we have. We'll catch you up." Her father gave her a hug and off Alice ran toward the orchard, leaving her parents smiling as they watched.

They saw her run across the garden, then slow to clap her hands to her mouth, to stand and stare. Alice's first thoughts were, who has put a shed in my orchard by my tree house. Then she looked down at the keys in her hand. She could see a padlock on the shed door.

'Mmmm', she thought. 'a tool shed for dad to use'.
She walked slowly now, up to the shed, smelling the freshness of new timber. Yes. The key fitted the padlock. Opening the door wide Alice went in to find an old school desk and a chair inside. No tools. On the desk was a large envelope with *'To Alice'* written across it. With fast beating heart she fumbled the envelope open to find a large card with *'Birthday Wishes'* written across it on a beautiful picture of primroses and violets. Inside it said *"Happy Birthday dear Alice, and Happy Easter. Hope you love your new den"*. It was signed *"Lots of love Mum, Dad & the two dogs."*

Alice sat down on the chair to read it all again. She reached out to touch the walls, then looked out of the window. She did not know whether to laugh or cry. Two dens. The old tree house and now this lovely shed. Her very own 'hut'. Across from her and looking towards her perched two little owls on the hawthorn tree by the fallen bullace tree.

That is where they live, she thought. And they know my new den. Alice leapt up and ran home, to find her mother and father making a cup of tea and smiling.

"This is my favouritest ever birthday, ever and ever", she cried, as they all hugged each other.
"The tree house can stay where it is Alice", her father said, " but I'll repair the ladder before you use it".
"Yes dad. I wont go up until it's done. Now I have lots to do in my new hut. I'll take a few of my books for the shelf."

Her mother chuckled. "You had better take that rug I fetched down from the attic too. It will fit nicely. I'll bring it over a bit later, you get your books."

Within the hour Alice was sitting at her desk, feet cosy in a thick sheepskin rug, watching across the orchard.

To her joy she could see straight across to where two little owls were taking food of some kind into the old hawthorn she called the Fairy Tree, from its gnarled and twisted shape and the way it held the ancient plum tree that had fallen years before.

Alice knew the owls had young. She knew birds did not continuously carry food to one place for themselves to eat, but to feed babies.

Now I have a new nest too, she grinned, and made notes in her notebook about her exciting day, resolving to get a sketch book and paints to begin painting all the plants and animals she saw in the orchard from now on.

It was Alice who named 'her' two little owls Grail and Athene. She could recognise them apart, knowing the one she had been watching for days as it held territory, the male. It was darker in plumage, the white flecks showing more clearly on its wings so Grail, he became, from her love of a book on King Arthur her grandfather had once given her. Then, looking in her bird book at little owls Alice saw that the species was named Athene noctua. She read that the little owl is the wise owl of Athene, Goddess of Wisdom, and thus she had named the female, Grail's mate, Athene, who was more of a browny-grey and easy to recognise.

Grail had watched the activity in the orchard whilst his mate fed their three young. He would warn her of any danger but there was none. Now the orchard was peaceful and quiet once again. He knew that Alice had arrived and was now back inside the new hut but he knew also that she did not present a threat in any way. Grail flew across the orchard to land on the hut roof, a new perch and vantage point from which to watch over his family.

Inside, Alice rubbed her hands together with delight. She had seen the owl cross the orchard and could now see its shadow upon the grass before her, the hut shadow cast forward by the shining sun. She saw the wings flutter, then the owl flew out to begin hunting again to feed his young.

What a holiday, she thought. My own den next to my old tree house. And Easter eggs, and owls eggs, and now the baby owls. She wondered how many but would not go to look as it might upset all the owls. She knew that eventually they would come out to learn to fly. She would see them from her den when the time was right.

Oh, and a blackbird with a beakful of worms and insects. More babies. She began to write in her notebook. Such a lot to write about. But it will all add to my home lessons in different ways, she thought happily to herself. Art, from sketching and painting, English and Earth Sciences from all I see. History and Geography from all past and present around and about the area, so that covers science as well. Reading of course. Dad and Mum always refer to the '3Rs' of their day. Reading, riting and rithmatic. Alice giggled to herself at the 3 Rs . What awful spellers people must have been in those days! Yes, her own home environment and the wonderful countryside all around, Dartmoor and Exmoor and beyond. They would be her classroom.

"Lunch is ready!"

Alice heard her mother's call. She looked around her new hut. Her new den. Easter. What a diary I am going to write, she thought, the best diary ever written in the whole world. And she went homewards across the orchard knowing she was watched by little owls.

Athene and Grail watched Alice leave her new hut. Immediately they increased their hunting of insects, mice and the occasional earthworm, feeding their young before themselves. The old orchard was ideal hunting ground for little owls, there being many field and wood mice available and even young brown rats for these were on the increase generally over the whole of the region.

The orchard hedge banks of soil and stone, planted with hawthorn, called quickset by the country people for it was the fastest growing hedge tree, was now beginning to blossom. May is out. The gentle lacy frothyness of cow parsley added its own paleness along with the splashes of primrose yellow, the purple of dog violet and gold of coltsfoot which had been blooming since February.

A cock pheasant called aloud 'kuk-kuk' as he patrolled the orchard edge, his mate sitting in the far corner well hidden by two russet apple trees. These and a few other pheasants had moved onto the farm having escaped a 'shoot' two years previously. Here they were as safe as any game bird on a non-shooting farm could be, even from the resident fox for foxes tend to hunt away from their home earths.

Pheasant chicks are not taken by little owls as had once been thought when the bird was introduced into the country during the 19th century and spread into every county in England in a short time. Not all little owls had arrived as introductions however. Athene's own ancestors had flown from the continent and established themselves well in Devon and Cornwall from these more natural origins.

But these things are not of interest to the owls, their thoughts are to survival, of living their lives. For three weeks Athene and Grail fed the young owls. All had grown well, the weather mostly kind and food abundant. In two or three days the young would be fully fledged. Already they looked like their parents, each fully feathered save for some down on one of the three's cheeks.

The two adults were tired but thriving. About the orchard beneath favourite roosting spots the pellets of regurgitated food remains showed beetles and some rodents were the main food taken, though many a moth flying at dusk had been caught by the adults. Earwigs, cockchafers, too, became part of the diet as spring time and the three young ones progressed and Alice's Easter holiday drew to an end.

Jacob Brown had taken to watching the little owls with Alice on one evening in the week and at weekends. Together the two had noted how the adult owls did not often take insects such as moths in flight but caught them on the ground or on the vegetation. Active hawking was rare they noticed and now, as the nestlings were close to fledging, it was amazing to watch them bobbing up and down as they peered out at the great, wide world they would soon inhabit.

Alice now had RSPB Bird Charts pinned to one wall of her new den and copious notes written in school type exercise books. In a large 200 page pad she was writing the details of 'her' little owls progress, along with other nests, the wildflowers, and butterflies that were about the orchard.

Her father had taken up photography again, finding his 35mm SLR camera in a cupboard. He had bought a 300mm lens for it and had already taken some pleasing shots of the little owls without causing them any disturbance.

Alice's mum had begun sowing wildflower seeds in beds at the front and back of the farmhouse, instead of the usual bedding plants and all in all the three were busy enjoying, observing and helping wildlife. "A common interest", Jacob had said to Mary as they lay in bed watching the Moon rise over the distant hill. "It has done Alice the world of good".
"And us too Jacob", smiled his wife. "And us too."

On the 33rd day from the hatching of her eggs Athene awoke to a mist shrouded morning, the trees of the orchard seeming to float on a cloud where usually there was grass and many daffodils. It was the Morning Pride of country people but Athene knew not of such things, knew only that she was hungry and there were three dozing young owls close by her in their tree hole lair.

Slight sounds caused her to turn her head on one side as she focussed sharp eyes to where Alice was just putting down her flask of tea and box of sandwiches, to quietly undo the padlock of her shed door and just as quietly go inside.

Athene watched the door close. Seeing Grail, her mate fly from his roost in the tree house she flew after him to the far end of the orchard where the morning mist was thinnest and barely obscured the ground. The two adult owls had hunted from dusk into the night, feeding the young on earwigs, woodlice, a house mouse and centipedes. So busy were they feeding the almost fully fledged nestlings, that neither had eaten. Now perched in a James Grieve apple tree the two surveyed the ground beneath them to find breakfast of some kind.

A fox crossed the orchard carrying one of the many rabbits living on and about the farm. The vixen had four cubs in an earth in the hedge bank adjoining the orchard, hungry mouths to feed and as she never bothered the farm livestock she was tolerated by Jacob Brown and his wife.

The vixen trotted beneath the owls, climbing the bank with her prize, dislodging loose soil as she did so. Several earthworms and beetles, exposed by her passing, were swiftly taken by Athene and Grail, pounced upon, eaten where they wriggled or ran.

Their hunger satisfied for the moment the two owls flew up onto the apple tree branch once again, Athene calling 'kiew' as she perched beside her mate. Then both owls called almost simultaneously and on the third such calling the first of the young launched towards his parents and with much fluttering dropped to the ground immediately beneath them.

In her shed-den Alice clapped her hands with glee. She had observed every move, even to the vixen passing through the orchard but this for her was magic. She had been allowed to get up very early and go to the den much earlier than usual as she had worked out when the young should fly to within a day or two and had struck very lucky indeed.

Alice took a bite from her bacon sandwich, her favourite, and drank some tea. She was excited and wanted to run out and hug the owls but knew that that was not a very good idea. Instead she made notes in what was now becoming more a book than a diary, recording the time of day the owl first flew, everything she could remember.

Athene dropped to the ground by her first hatched son, as Grail flew about the orchard calling, then alighted on a branch by the other two young ones, another male and a female. By 10 O'clock that morning the two adults had flown several times about the orchard, sometimes following the young one, sometimes with fledged bird in hot pursuit.

It was not until 2 O'clock in the afternoon that the second male flew to join his brother at the end of the orchard and by 2.30pm the young female was out on the branch below their nest hole. Alice's parents watched from the lane so as not to disturb the birds unduly. They had left a picnic container behind the shed and Alice had opened the rear window to receive it. She was learning that such birds may leave the nest to fly free with half a day between them and indeed it was at 6pm in the evening when the female left her perch to circle the orchard twice then hurtle to the roof of Alice's den.

Mary looked at her husband.

"I reckon we ought to celebrate all this at dinner tonight Jacob", she said. "You see if you can get a few photos without upsetting the owls. I've put a roast in the oven so seven O'clock sharp and us'll open a bottle of that elder flower wine we made".

"Sounds good to me maid. I'll see Alice is at the table well in time. This has been quite an Easter!"

Trevor Beer's FIVE OWLS

3

Strix - The Tawny Owl

Prologue

"If it is my pleasure when I sing to refuse all other dwellings, I have still in the woods some mighty trees, with thick bows that are never bare, covered over with ivy that is ever in leaf, and evergreen whether it snows or freezes.

And there I have a splendid stronghold, warm in winter, in summer cool; and when that dwelling stands bright and green, then of thine is nothing seen".

'The Owl and the Nightingale'.
Anon. (13th century.)

Chapter 1

It had been raining steadily. One of those days when the whole region was enveloped in greyness and water, fields under water and filled with water fowl and gulls instead of sheep and cattle, for the grazing was waterlogged. Water. The word was on everyone's lips as meteorologists and weather forecasters spoke or wrote of the wettest autumn and winter 'since records began', which in reality was but a moment in time.

But it was now the first week of the February month. In the fields below the steeply wooded hillside almost a hundred frogs were croaking and mating, the noise of their frolicking heard from a quarter of a mile radius to those with good ears.

There were few with better hearing than Strix, the tawny owl, or those of her kind. Their whole existence was based on their ability to hear and then to directionise upon the sounds, upon the slightest movement, the rustling and squeaking of tiny mammals, the shifting of leaves and twigs, the sighting of a breeze through branches, the splashes of a trout in the nearby weir pool.

It was dimmity time. Owl light as locals called it. The time of purple shadows lengthening across the fields at sunset, when from the hollow tree where Strix lived, the tree bark all about turned pink or red, or sometimes gold depending on the intensity of the sinking sun colour. It is at such moments that all the senses of owls awaken, as bats fly out from day roosts to waylay insects and eat their kill.

A fox moved out from the shadows of a small quarry close to the wood entrance, to pass beneath Strix silently perched in her oak tree lair. The fox was Old Red the dog fox who lived in the woods. Strix watched him trot along by the hedgerow filled with the gold stars of lesser celandines and then he was gone. Strix knew he would head for the easy hunting grounds of Shearford Lane and the rabbit fields along the waterway for she often found him about when she too, was hunting, the lane giving much shelter to many wildlife species whilst at the same time providing a larder of abundance by day or night.

But Strix heard the splashing of brown trout in the leat. Three days before seven of them had washed into the weir pool from the main stream, forced by the current, forced by the power of water that had poured into their usually peaceful pool, turning it into a place of difficult currents.

In recent times water bailiffs of the Environment Agency, the former National Rivers Authority, had spent a minute portion of their budget to create a 'salmon leap' of sand bags to help the fish penetrate to breeding redds further upstream. The fish had always used the waterway but the weir could be a formidable barrier to their progress and the sand bag 'salmon leap' helped them on their way. It was ever the way of it for salmon coming home to their birth rivers. They could reach the coast to seek out their river mouths by remembered scent and taste, then lie in wait for rains that would swell the waterways. With the rushing of 'fresh' out into the sea the great fish move in as a 'run' to seek out the gravely redds well inland but where there were weirs and waterfalls, the very rains that called them in from the sea, were the powerful cascades that fought their progress and penetration of the rivers and streams.

But the brown trout knew not the seas and oceans. They remained in the fresh water throughout their lives, as much to the river and streams as Strix and her kind are to the woods and lanes, the trees and the wildflowers of the land.

From her oak tree perch Strix flew to the branch of an ash by the leat side, water drops falling from the rain sodden young ash leaves catching the light from a half moon now visible through wind blown clouds. The owl heard the pattering of the raindrops, heard the croaking of frogs along the leat, heard, too, the splash of one of the trout in the weir pool. She was hungry. Constant rains had kept the small mammal population in their runs and burrows to a large extent so hunting had been poor.

Many thousands of lesser celandines bunched along both sides of the leat and weir pool. Even closed to the night they showed the line of the ancient waterway. Strix saw silver forms in the shallows where a narrow path used by poachers led from the field edge to the waterway.

Strix dropped to the lowest branch above the water, the only sound he made, that of sharp talons seeking a foothold but it was a sound not heard above the roar of the weir. Head slightly on one side Strix gazed down upon the trout, all with their heads to the bank and facing slightly upstream. The fish were as silver in the blackness of the water and as Strix watched, the trout furthest upstream of the others allowed itself to drift back from the bank into deeper water. It had seen the dark shape arrive above it knowing it well from three days and nights spent in the weir pool.

The second brown trout in line gently flicked its tail to drift back into deeper water with the first to move but as the third made to follow so the owl was upon it, gripping fiercely as she felt water splash her legs and the talons of her other foot rake the back of another trout.

Then Strix was up on beating wings, her prey wriggling slightly as lifted from its life giving water it felt its strength ebbing in the vice-like owl grip. Up onto the main wood path Strix flew and holding the trout down with her talons she mantled the prey beneath half open wings, tearing hungrily at her meal.

Strix had learned to catch fish. From now on this skill would be a part of her remembered hunting methods both as fancy and the stimulus of splashing trout takes her, and when times were difficult and hunger is the spur, as is the way of wild creatures.

Chapter 2

Mattie Jameson looked from her cottage window, glancing across the garden to the stream and the woods beyond. It was the month of May. She loved May and June but June with its midsummer madness of wildflowers, grasses, birdsong and insects was her absolute favourite month. It was a humming, buzzing and active month filled with young birds recently fledged, vying with the adults in their flying, flitting and flowing through the air or along the stream. She sighed. And how she loved May, and all the months she grinned.

She stood with a mug of tea in one hand, scrunching on well done toast, butter and marmalade held in the other, relaxed in her favourite bottle green towelling dressing gown. A grey wagtail flew up from the stream bank and back again, catching insects now abundant and lively in the 10am morning sunshine.

Mattie was having a week's holiday. As a freelance writer and artist she could not afford what some would call real holidays but to her, where better than her own remote cottage in the Devon countryside. Her own little bit of heaven. There was nowhere better on Earth. So she was having 'a break' to recharge her batteries as she put it, though she loved her rather precarious lifestyle and would not change it for the world.

With her parents retired and living in Cornwall, Mattie lived in the cottage left to her by her beloved maternal grandparents some ten years previously. At 30 she was as successful as a good Westcountry writer and wildlife artist can be, selling articles and the occasional painting to put food on the table and pay the bills.

As she was sipping the last of her tea and contemplating pouring another, a car pulled up by her front gate. She watched as an elderly man and woman got out, the woman opening the gate to let the man into the garden, carrying what looked like a bundled towel. Mattie recognised them from the nearby village though she did not know them other than to wave and smile hello.

Pulling her dressing gown belt tight about her pyjamas Mattie went to the front door just as the couple arrived in her porch. The man, with what Mattie saw was in fact a bundled towel spilling from a box, smiled at her.

"Er, Miss Jameson I believe. This is all most awkward but I have an owl in the box which seems oily. We found it by the garage entrance a mile back the road and knowing you lived here and love owls I wonder if you could take it in?"

The man rushed through his little speech apprehensively, standing with a worried look on his face.

"Well I do love owls but how did you know? And why to me? Oh and do come in to the kitchen. Is the owl likely to get out?"

The woman chimed in.

"Oh no. We're the North's at the Old Forge. The owl is safely held but in need of help. We know you love owls because I brought my husband one of your delightful owl paintings. It is so lovely you just must really love them as we do. Your exhibition in the village hall about two years ago. Do you remember? It was Richard's birthday that week and he so loved your painting. It is in his study."

Mattie remembered. She had sold half a dozen paintings and recalled the owl well, a tawny owl picture she had enjoyed doing.

"Oh yes. So you have a May birthday Mr. North. But we had better look at this owl, I'm no vet". She smiled, taking the box gingerly and placing it on a newspaper she slowly opened the towel back.

From the seclusion of the deep box two gleaming dark eyes gazed into hers and Mattie heard the click of the owls beak as she stared.

"Oh my. It is a tawny owl and so beautiful, and oh my, so oily. However did that happen I wonder?"

"Well, we can only think it fell into oil at the garage yard, then found its way out onto the roadside. I saw it on the grass verge as Richard slowed in case a vehicle was coming out. They often do there you know." Mrs.North stared worriedly into the box.

"Yes, I know the repair garage. I suppose it isn't open on a Saturday. Looks as if we ought to clean the owl. I'll put things ready".

She remembered her father cleaning an oiled bird once some years previously. Quite warm water and liquid dish washing soap he'd used, and he had kept the bird until it was well, for a few days.

Mattie busied herself with more newspapers and towels, telling the couple she was on a week's holiday which was fortuitous.

"The spare bedroom. I have two", she said "I'll keep him there. Oh I wonder why I think it is a him?" She smiled. "Mr.North could you pop upstairs and open the second door on the landing and close the window in that room for me please."

"Richard, call me Richard. And this is Geraldine. I think it's a male owl. He looks a solemn sort of chap like me don't you think?" Humming he went off upstairs as Mattie carefully closed the kitchen door and window.

She poured hot water into an old bowl she kept for odd jobs, mixing in the 'Fairy Liquid' and cold water until the water was just hand hot.

"Now. Gardening gloves. Those talons look rather sharp

Mr.Owl. That's it, now let us have a look at you."

Mattie lifted the bird easily from its box, placing it on the towel and paper on the table as Mrs.North watched.

"Oh it is not so bad at all. Only on the chest from what I can see. What a relief. I know what has happened. The oil is cloggy and heavy. The owl is over its flying weight. I remember my father telling me about such things years ago. Just a touch too heavy and birds are grounded. The right weight is all very critical."

Richard North returned to the kitchen. "All set my dear. Shall we stay? Do you need a hand?"

Mattie smiled. "No. Not being rude but it may be better if you left. Less people, less stress for the bird I think. But leave your phone number on the pad there by the phone and I will let you know how things go."

"I think you are right", Geraldine North replied as her husband wrote their telephone number and asked. "We will go on to town to do our shopping. Is there anything we can get you while we are there dear?"

Mattie now had the owl firmly held with one hand though it struggled powerfully, clicking its beak loudly.

"Well, I have meat in the freezer but it'll be rock hard. I wonder if you could pick up some meat, or maybe there is a rabbit hanging in the shop, something fresh I can give him please?"

"No sooner said than done, some fresh meat it shall be, and good luck with your spring cleaning". Richard North grinned, ushering his wife from the cottage and along the path to the road.

Mattie heard their car drive away as she soaked an old face flannel in the warm, soapy liquid and began to gently but firmly clean the owl's breast feathers. She found the standing position difficult so sitting on a chair she laid the owl on its back along her legs, its head at her knees. She gazed into its dark blackberry eyes as she worked, smiling at the bird, feeling it tensing and relaxing at her touch.

"What are you thinking Woody? Yes I'll call you Woody just in case you are a female. It's a name that suits either sex don't you think? You must be wondering whatever is happening to you, you poor thing."

The owl stared back at her as she chatted away, his eyes occasionally closing, then opening suddenly again and Mattie could sense the power in the owl and knew she must treat every move with utmost care. She glanced down at the black talons, shivering momentarily, seeing them close then distend.

Mattie had read many books about wildlife and her father had taken her on countless country walks, telling her of the wild creatures and plants they saw, and of past times and the memories of his own boyhood in the countryside.

The owl clicked its beak loudly and struggled one wing free, flapping it powerfully so that Mattie could feel the wind in her face.

"Goodness you are a strong fellow", she said, holding on and using a towel with downward strokes to dry the owl's now clean feathers.

"There that's taken us half an hour and you have been very good. Now I am going to take you upstairs to rest and settle down. You'll have a meal later and then we'll see how you are my Woody friend."

The owl freed his other wing and began to flap both, lifting his tawny body fiercely as he struggled against Mattie's grip.

She felt talons grip one of her gloves as the owl's wings beat faster. For a moment she felt frightened then she managed to hold its two legs in one hand. Bringing its wings to its body with the other Mattie hurried upstairs and putting the owl down on the spare bed she quickly went out and closed the door.

Good heavens, she thought. Am I doing the right thing to keep it a while? The owl had felt so strong she felt maybe she should have freed it immediately. Then, no. Be sure it's had some food first. Will it eat? And it is very sunny and daylight, not a tawny owl's best time of day.

Mattie realised she was trembling ever so slightly. A cup of tea, then clean up. Heavens I'm not dressed yet. But me and the owl have both had baths. She grinned. All would be alright she knew. She went quickly downstairs hearing a crash from the owl's room. She chuckled. That'll be the pink and blue vase she never really liked receiving a blow from the owl.

An hour later Mattie was dressed in shirt and cord jeans,

having a cup of strong tea.

She strolled out into the garden, loving the lawn with its daisies. Looking up to the cottage windows she could see the owl perched on the sill, half closed eyes gazing sombrely down at her. She could not resist a wave but the owl, Woody, she liked the name, closed his eyes fully against the daylight and dozed.

Mattie sat on her garden seat beneath her one Bramley apple tree, watching the tawny owl sleep. What an odd morning she thought, I must phone mum and dad later and tell them all about it. And paint more owl pictures. She remembered the North's would be coming back and decided to prepare a plate piled high with sandwiches, and to have the kettle on.

Somewhere between noon and 1pm the North's arrived back, bustling along the cottage pathway with two shopping bags.

"Got your meat, well the owl's meat. Told the butcher what it was for and he cut up some bits and pieces and sent them with his compliments, for the owl". Richard North beamed.

"And we have brought you some fruit to say thank you my dear", Geraldine North added, putting the bulky bag she was carrying on the kitchen table. "And how's our dear friend?"

Mattie smiled. "Absolutely fine. He is dozing but you can see him from the garden as we eat our sandwich lunch and swig tea. What do you think? It's lovely out".

"Excellent. We'd love to wouldn't we dear", Richard North said to his wife. "Oh, and if you get around to painting a barn owl to match my tawny owl picture then we would be truly pleased to commission it please".

"Lovely. Of course I'd be pleased. So sit over there in the garden while I make tea. Wont be long".

And so two hours flew by as the three enjoyed their snack lunch, watching the tawny owl at the same time. Mattie told the North's that she realised feeding the owl was more down to the owl wanting to eat than to her wanting to feed it and in any case the bird was not sick or injured and was probably only too ready to go.

"It'll be getting dimmity around 7ish", Mattie said. "I think that is the time to test the situation to see if Woody is ready to fly free again".

"Then may we pop back to watch?" Richard North asked.

"Or better still, stay. It'll be no trouble to knock up some omelettes. Do you like a nice, thick omelette, I have plenty of eggs. Real dinner plate size".

It was agreed. Mattie went indoors, took some of the chopped meat upstairs and quietly let herself in to the spare room. The tawny owl started as she went in and as she quickly closed the door, heart beating rapidly the bird turned its large head round without moving its body, to gaze solemnly and wide-eyed at her.

In for a penny, she thought. Walking casually to the window she put the meat on the wide sill by the owl, turned and walked away out of the room.

That's the best I can do she decided as she walked back down stairs after washing her hands. At least the owl appeared docile enough, and she could soon clean the paintwork.

The North's agreed things seemed to be going very well. Mattie showed them how she worked, and a few sketches and paintings she had done. Then by 7 O'clock, zero hour as Richard North called it, they had enjoyed dinner, washed up and the little cottage was again spick and span.

"Now I'm going to do something daft but hopeful." Mattie jumped up. "I am going to put the remainder of this meat down on the roof of my large bird table at the end of the garden. I doubt that Woody will notice it but he or she, I'm sure he's a he, just might and it is the best we can do, to make sure there's food available."

She took the remainder of the meat across the garden and carefully placed it on the bird table roof. Glancing up she could see the owl crouched on the window sill as the setting sun cast a golden glow over the cottage and garden. It was one of Mattie's favourite moments of the day. And what a day she thought, two new friends, no, three. She looked up again to find Woody standing upright, gazing down at her as she walked towards her home.

"Right. This is the right moment I think. Do watch from the lounge window. I'm going straight up to open the window of Woody's room and stand back".

"Good luck dear, and good luck to the owl too," Geraldine North said.

Mattie hurried upstairs, listening outside the spare bedroom. There was no sound from inside. Carefully she opened the door to find Woody staring at her from the sill.

"You know it's time to go don't you", she said, then gasped. Just one piece of the meat remained on the sill and there was none on the floor below.

"You've had dinner too. What a wonderful thing. Now let me open the window".

She leaned forward to release the catch, seeing the owl half open its wings as it also leaned against the glass. In the very second of the window swinging outwards so the owl was away, out over the garden where it circled once then flew to the trees at the edge of the woods beyond.

Mattie was misty-eyed but very happy. She heard a cheer from below and watched enthralled as the owl landed to perch on an oak branch facing her.

"Bye Woody", she called gently. "And thanks for a lovely day".

If she had not seen the owl land she would never have realised it was there on the branch, so much a part of the woods had it become. But as she went back downstairs Mattie knew she would look for 'her owl' each day and night, and hope to see it yet again.

"Amazing m'dear. All's well and all that. We had a fine day, a lovely day. Now we must be off home. But don't forget that painting. And where we live".

The North's said their goodbyes and drove away home. Mattie stood in the garden, the scent of the May evening almost heady as a blackbird began singing its last song to the day.

Then she heard it. 'Kee-wick, kee-wick', and she waved to the sound, knowing she could not see it. 'Kee-wick, kee-wick'. It called again and she went back in doors to pour a glass of wine to drink to all of nature and the good things in her life.

Chapter 3

Early evening mist had cloaked the pasture fields and meadows below the wooded hillside, the paleness writhing inexorably into the woods at the height of a badgers back, rendering hunting visibility difficult.

The badgers, living in an ancient sett at the western edge of the woods had fed on earthworms found in plenty on the hill slope adjoining the tree line. They had fed from sunset until the crescent moon rose high with Jupiter shining brightly then they had lumbered home, trooping back along a well worn path beneath a barbed wire fence to their sett. One, a wily old boar, had eaten a mole which had been earth throwing a mole hill into the field at the very moment the badger had scraped the loose mound for worms.

Somewhere a farm dog barked as the fox who lived in an earth at the top of the woods trotted amongst hazel trees up along a path worn by his own regular passing. He carried a mallard duck in his jaws, caught roosting with six others who had flown in from the marshes adjoining the estuary, the previous night.

The dog fox trotted faster, his mouth watering for fresh duck, knowing he was closer to his lair and he would not need to hunt for two or three days for the bird was plump and heavy.

Above him as he reached his earth a tiny slate grey and buff bird with sharp beak and masked eyes raised its sleep filled head. Then, tucking it beneath one wing, the nuthatch went back to sleep on five eggs laid on dead oak leaves in a tree hole made by a green woodpecker two years before. Now with her clutch fully laid she would rest and incubate the eggs for two weeks whilst her mate brought her food each day. They had raised six young the previous year in the same nest hole, the opening made by the woodpeckers reduced in size by the nuthatches with mud brought from the nearby stream and mill leat.

The scrunch of fox jaws biting through duck flesh and bones carried to the ears of Strix who gazed down wide-eyed to the fox earth below her perch in a hollow ash tree. She disgorged a pellet which hit the ground and rolled amongst the wild garlic growing in a dense row alongside the fox path and bluebells but not amongst them. There were many tawny owl pellets hidden by the bright green leaves and stems of the white flowered plant of the onion family, pellets of skulls, bones and fur of small mammals, and of beetles elytra and fish scales regurgitated by the owl.

Strix had moved to the top of the woods, finding the ash tree hollow to her liking after fine spring days began to bring too many people, and dogs along the bottom path of the woods. She did not like daytime noise when she was sleeping and few people came to the top of the woods for the slope was steep and brambles as thick as men's fingers and thumbs clambered across what few paths there were.

Now Strix gazed from her high perch, across a large field to where a light shone from farm buildings almost half a mile away as an owl flies. Strix could hear nothing below her that suggested food for herself. Even the sounds of the feeding fox had ceased for with stomach filled he dozed with his white chin on duck feathers. Strix fidgeted from one foot to the other then launching from the ash branch she flew with rapid wing beats low across the field. Seeing movement below her she checked for but a moment, hovering to see a hedgehog trotting towards the trees, then rising slightly she flew on towards the light and the outline of dark, shadowy buildings that was the farmstead.

Reaching the farm the owl dropped to perch on a wooden gate leaning into a yard lined along one side by outbuildings. She could see the barn where she knew two sheepdogs lay snugly asleep together in hay each night. Once they had awoke to the sound of her dropping upon a mouse near where they lay and their barking had frightened her enough to have her drop her supper.

But Strix could see movement beneath the security light above the largest of the three outbuildings, the hump-shaped form of a brown rat gnawing at an apple put out for birds to eat. Strix tensed for flight as the apple, set in motion by the rat's movements rolled across the slightly sloping yard towards her with the rat following it with its wobbling trotting motion, eager to eat the fruit. With a bound the rat reached the escaping apple then screaming it died as fierce talons pierced and held its writhing body in a vice-like grip.

Four eyes saw the tawny owl rise from the ground with a large rat dangling beneath it and four eyes closed again as the two collies, used now to the hunting of owls by night, and hawks by day, huddled closer and went back to sleep.

Strix carried her prey away from the farm, back across the field, locating her ash tree home where she was soon eating her fill. Below her a fox tucked his head deeper beneath his tail, eyes tight closed, listening to a rising wind moaning through the treetops.

Chapter 4

The wind blew moaning across the land for two days and nights, even stilling the songs of chiff chaffs and willow warblers here to breed for the summer. They silently went about the business of feeding up and resting. Their nest sites chosen, many from the previous year or two, these warblers often seek and find the very nest hollows used before, a metre of ground, in a wood, after thousands of miles of travel from Africa.

At the farm where Strix sometimes hunted, swallows were already at old, established nesting sites in the barns where the farmer allowed them constant access each year. In an earth bank of the river below the woods, kingfishers were with eggs in a tunnel hacked from the soil in April.

Strix, who disliked the wind, spent the two days with her head down below the lip of the ash tree hollow, dozing. The lair had been formed when a huge branch had snapped and fallen to the woodland floor below, for the tree was old. In its falling away the branch had left a cavity which in the course of time had weathered to what was now a timber cavern, dry and spacious enough for Strix to clamber into and move about with ease. Moreover a hole at the side of the ash bole gave views over the immediate terrain and thus, for Strix, the advantage of knowing much of what was occurring around and about her.

On the second night of moaning wind heavy rain fell, blowing in from the south west. To the owl in the ash tree, the fox in his hedgerow earth and the kingfishers in their tunnel in the river bank the down pour was but an inconvenience but to many creatures it spelled much danger.

Come morning moorhens on the former millpond by the leat where Strix once caught trout, toiled to raise their nest higher as the leat over flowed into the pond. The female moorhen had laid the first two eggs of her spring clutch but the water level had risen to lap against them and she would have to begin a fresh clutch upon her new platform.

Beneath the single arched stone bridge dippers watched anxiously as rushing water rose to almost touch their own nest with its four young whilst fifty human paces further down stream a pair of grey wagtails flew along the bank in vain as their nest of six nestlings was washed away from its bank side crevice. They flew to the stile bridge calling 'chisick-chisick' only to see the nest debris sweep under the wooden structure but of their young there was no sign.

The wagtails flew back upstream, seeing the dippers busily feeding their young. With the stimulus still deep within them from days of feeding their own nestlings they began to catch insects, taking them to the young dippers whose open gapes hungered for food with no concern or awareness of who fed them. The two adult dippers continued to feed their kind as across the field watching, an excited naturalist noted the incident with great care.

With the ceasing of the rain a buzzard flew out from the trees to seek food for his two young and his mate. He had perched with her on opposite sides of their stick nest, their open wings mantling over the two downy white nestlings to keep them dry in the darkness of the night. At dawn, stiff, cold and wet he had shaken himself free of water, touched his weary mates bill with his own and launched from the nest side to find food.

Strix, hearing his 'peeoo' calls opened her eyes to watch him fly through the trees and out over the valley, then she dozed again, snug in her tree hole. The buzzard flew low, his wing beats deep, his sharp eyes watching for movement that may mean food. He followed the stream down the valley, the water yellow with rain, passing over a grey heron standing hunched by the footbridge used by walkers.

Sheep with lambs were in the hillside, but there were none dead and the buzzard flew on coming to the mill leat where he turned, flying higher, screaming 'pee-ooo' loud so that his mate knew he was hunting. Below him movement from a hawthorn hedgerow was the first grass snake out of hibernation, writhing sinuously to where a toad sat above the mill waterfall. With its first meal for the year firmly in its sights the snake saw the shadow of the buzzard grow large upon the grass then it was clasped behind the head and lifted high, writhing and wriggling, in the hawks talons.

Away over two fields the grass snake flew, to be brought to the branch holding the buzzard's nest in its fork with the tree trunk. It feigned death in the manner of grass snakes then died as the female buzzard, bigger and heavier than her mate, dealt it blows about the head with partly opened bill. She tore meat from its now still body for her young, feeding them both before taking food for herself. Her hunger gone she called to her mate, settling down with her two chicks, her body feeling the warmth of the sun as her mate devoured his own share of the snake. Once fed he flew to a branch in the next tree to watch his mate pull ivy onto and about the nest, decorating it with the camouflaging plant, the grass snake remains lying upon the nest for another meal.

Below them a female small tortoiseshell butterfly laid her eggs beneath the terminal shoot of a stinging nettle as a male blackcap sang its song from a shrub where his mate sat on five tiny eggs in a nest they had built together. The male buzzard dozed, occasionally opening his eyes to see his mate and two young on the nest as nearby Strix the tawny owl waited for darkness.

Dusk time, the dimmity of Westcountry folk, owl-light as some say. Strix was alert, a scramble and two wing beats had taken her to a branch above her favourite roost and now she looked down upon the sunset's glow on bluebells carpeting the woodland floor. Gradually they showed deep purple then began to blend into shadowy darkness as the white of wild garlic flowers strengthened in the gathering gloom, showing the line of the fox path amongst the trees.

The night was warm and still, the woodland dark beneath the canopy of spring leaves, the sound of the distant weir muted, the song of a blackcap piercing the night.

Strix launched from her perch, following the pale line of wild garlic down to a huge fallen oak lying by the glinting waterway chattering its way to the weir pool. She perched briefly on the great roots of the fallen tree, hearing wood mice scamper amongst the soil and loose stones now sprouting hart's tongue fern and wood sorrel for the tree had fallen ten years before. She saw movement by the weir, and hearing human voices she screeched aloud to fly on out over the open field.

"Bleddy owls!" A man said disgruntledly to his companion. "Made me jump out me skin."
"Me too. Still these two salmon will fetch a few quid and the money'll steady our nerves". He carefully shone a torch, the light, covered by slightly opened fingers glowing blood red and white, showing where two fine fish lay on the stream bank.
"Aye. They'm good fish. This late spring run id'n too bad at all thanks to that rain".
"Too true Reg. We've done well what with they elvers early on but they bailiffs take some watching don't em."
"Aye," Reg answered. "But they can't be everywhere any more'n us can and with Philip watchin the only way in with ee's bird whistle ready, that was a good idea of 'is".
"Too true Reg. Let's get a move on".

The poachers, with a ten pound salmon each, now in hessian sacks, moved quietly away from the weir and over the stone single arched bridge. They did not short cut across the open field but held to the hedgerow around its perimeter, their dark clothing and black balaclavas rendering them virtually invisible.

Reaching the bottom of a tree lined lane which led for a quarter of a mile to a road they found their third man, Philip, waiting.

"All clear", he whispered. "Now I'll plod up the lane with a bit of noise and you two cut up over the field t'other side of the hedge and wait up top til I get there and see the coast is clear". He chuckled. "They can't grumble at me for gwane out badger watching".

The men parted and were soon at the road which was empty and silent in both directions.

"Right Reg, go". Philip said, and they watched Reg silently cross the road to the iron kissing gate entrance to another footpath which led towards the town.

"Now you Alan", and the second poacher disappeared after the first with his salmon.

A low whistle and Philip followed, all three moving in line along the dark pathway then down steps to the roadway and a modern housing estate where the salmon went into the boot of a parked car.

"A good night's work boys", Philip grinned as he drove them homeward through the night. "A good night's work".

In a horse chestnut tree at the roadside a tawny owl perched. He had eaten two voles taken easily on the neatly mown grass circle upon which the tree grew. Once the tree had grown in the centre of a pasture field but new development had urbanised the area with dwellings and roads named after composers of classical music, the tree standing isolated at the road end.

The owl had flown but two miles from the woods where two days before he had landed in oil in a garage yard and had then been tended by humans and released. His recollections of the incident were already scattered upon the wind but on the second day following his cleaning and release he had flown again to hunt the empty garage site. He had smelt again the stench of oil, some stirring in his owl mind warning him of danger and he had flown higher over the building, then on along the wood edge beneath a starlit sky, to follow a waterway to an old mill. Here he had been chased by two barn owls along a lane where they had suddenly left him at a road where blinding flashes of light were from a stream of vehicles.

Momentarily blinded he had flown to crash onto the galvanised iron roof of an allotment shed where he had remained perched, regaining his vision. Before him was a high hedge dividing the allotments and houses, behind him noise and flashing lights so the owl flew forward, soaring low above trim gardens and rooftops and thence to the lone horse chestnut tree, below which he caught two bank voles.

"Kee-wick, kee-wick", he called into the night, then was silent as the poachers appeared below him. He stared down upon them until they were gone with a roar of sound and lights which hurt his eyes. Again his sight adjusted to the darkness and again he called "kee-wick" calls into the night.
"Tu-whooo-hoo-ooo".

The tawny owl named Woody by the woman who had cleaned and fed him two days before, turned his head towards the northward darkness and the answering call of another owl.
"Kee-wick-kee-wick", he called, the sounds sharp upon the spring time air sending terror into bank voles leaping and scampering beneath him.

"Tu-whooo-oo". The low cry, mournful to the ears of man but striking joy into the heart of the questing male owl, came again.

"Kee-wick". He called once more then flew from his perch to wing his way along the route travelled by the poachers. Here at the lane top a stand of beech trees stood large before him, branches stretching silver and black towards the night sky.
"Tu-whoo-oo". He heard the call, seeing the dark silhouette of Strix perched upon a beech branch at the same moment. He alighted by her, waiting. Strix preened the feathers at the leading edge of one wing then gazed at him, calling again but softer now.

She left the perch, flying to another tree a little further down the lane, with Woody following. Again she flew, and again the male owl followed and then they were on the wing together, flying over the valley and its waterway, over the leat and weir to perch side by side at Strix's ash tree home.

Epilogue

The following spring the two tawny owls raised three young in the ash tree at the top of the woods exactly as I have described. The flight into the nest hole was downwards, typical of the species where such sites are available. The young hatched in April and flew in May after 29 days incubation and five weeks of fledging though they were observed about the nest somewhat before that time, as downy young.

I felt it necessary at 3 weeks into incubation to pull a fallen tree over the slightly noticeable 'path' up to the nest site and to train brambles all over it to obstruct the way as it was becoming overused. I found two youths attempting to reach a buzzard nest one evening and had to send them packing.

The poaching incident is as described except for where they parked their vehicle. The names used are ones I chose.

All three young flew successfully. There is a pair of tawny owls at this site now, ringing the changes on two nests, the ash tree site and a chimney type nest box I erected some years ago.

Mattie is a real lady.

Trevor Beer's FIVE OWLS

4

Asio & Hootlet
A Tale of Long-eared Owls

Chapter 1

Bitter northerly winds had moaned and howled across the Scottish Highlands for ten days, bringing snow and ice to the land, even freezing solid the smaller waterfalls of the region with their cold breath and the chilling sound as of wolves howling.

Highland red deer moved down from the hills and mountain sides to lower lying farmsteads as otters left frozen lochs and inland waterways to fish in the warmer sea but even they are forced to bathe the salt from their coats in freshwater coastal cascades.

Within the dense forests of the Ladder Hills, Scottish wildcats laid up lean and hungry for smaller mammal food was hard to find, the blizzards even penetrating the unbrashed forest trees.

Thus it was, on a night when a half moon turned the white landscape silver and black, Asio and Hoolet, two long-eared owls who had mated the previous summer, gazed at each other as a last flurry of snow heralded a brief respite. The cold northerly still moaned and the owls were hungry. Simultaneously launching from their adjacent perches in a larch tree, flying south carried by the wind gusts, no longer able to cope with the severe cold and hunger wrought by winter, they flew over the white wilderness which lay below and all about. Salmon and trout lay dead, frozen in ice in the rivers below them as they went, following streams to the Spey River.

On they flew over Loch an Eilean, the lake of the island, with its bleak ruins of the stronghold of Alexander, the Wolf of Badenoch, a place of ospreys in summer, and strange echoes. Then on, over Rothiemurchus Forest to eventually reach Loch Einich, a long narrow sheet of water, icy now at 1600 feet above the sea, towered over by the rocky ridge of Scoran Dubh, and containing salmon, trout and char.

But the two owls did not rest, flying on, Hoolet following close behind her mate, onward to the Forest of Atholl, where weary and hungry they rested by the Falls of Bruar. Here the weather was less fierce, the two owls each catching brown rats scavenging about a farmstead, the rats themselves lean and hungry, dying swiftly in the desperate vice-like grip of owl talons.

Their hunger satisfied the two owls rested close together, Hoolet on a perch leaning against a tree trunk, Asio leaning against her, their combined warmth staying them through the day. Nought moved in the forest, even the red squirrels remaining in their dreys though they were not hibernators. At night fall, as gentle rain fell upon the forest trees, once again the two long eared owls raised their ear tufts, gazed into each others fiery red eyes and launched southwards.

Through Dumfries and Galloway flew the two owls, eating voles caught at a dog kennels compound on one windy night, not heeding the barking of dogs, intent only on hunting and feeding. If there is a wisdom in owls it is the inherent intelligence to survive against the odds, and Asio and Hoolet were survivors.

To Annan they flew, finding ice at this narrow point of the Solway Firth, where over a century before, floating ice had smashed the railway viaduct connecting the market town to the Cumberland coast. The owls flapped and glided the mile and a half across the river which groaned beneath them as the freezing ice rubbed together as it piled against the banks, the northerly wind carrying them on into Cumbria, to Haweswater Reservoir. Here the owls rested and ate for two days and nights until the wind veered north-westerly and they followed the eastern side of the M6 motorway for all its length.

Asio and Hoolet ate each night now, a further week of flying bringing them close to Hereford, to follow the Severn Valley to the west of the M5. Where the River Teme joins the Severn they stayed a whole day, eating mice on a farm at Powick during the night. The two owls had regained their strength, England's winter less fierce than the weather they had left behind in Scotland.

Two nights of food and hard flying brought them into the Vale of Gloucester, then to the Severn Noose where they left the great river to cross the Vale of Berkely and the M5 motorway, following the Little Avon River southwards through Avon, to reach Chew Valley Lake nestling at the base of the Mendip Hills.

Here large numbers of wintering wildfowl were present and humans bird-watched about the lake. Asio and Hoolet found trees near the Hollow Brook inlet and here they perched together, warmer than they had been throughout the whole of their journey. Several birdwatchers saw the two long eared owls, recording them in their notebooks with some excitement as Asio and Hoolet gazed solemnly down upon them from their new found resting place.

That night the two owls took a jay, just before dusk as it flew into the trees to roost, then caught a rat scurrying by a stone wall who had paused to examine the carcase of a dead greenfinch. They thus ate well, and on the second day at Chew, found wood mice seeking caches of winter food stored in the old nests of blackbirds.

News of the long eared owls circulated amongst local bird watchers, who came to observe at a distance, the owls remaining for three days, building up their strength. Then for some reason known only to owls and other creatures of the wild, Asio and Hoolet left Chew Valley Lake to follow once more the southward route that had brought them out of Scotland many days before.

Crossing the Bruce River they flew south-west, reaching the village of Middlezoy in Somerset and then Westonzoyland where they hunted in the dusk, finding many mice on an old RAF Camp which had once been part of Bomber Command during the 1950s.

The next night saw them crossing the Vale of Taunton Deane, to eventually reach the River Taw near the small village of King's Nympton, where the two owls found dense forestry woodlands close to a large weir. Though cold, the Devonshire countryside between Dartmoor and Exmoor was relatively warm, snow falling on the two moorland National Parks but not upon the lower lying farmland.

Here by a popular salmon fishing weir Asio and Hoolet rested in a tree beside a high wall, with a cottage nearby wherein lived a Wildfowl Trust employee, the land belonging to that organisation.

At two O'clock of the morning on a night well lit by the moon the owls heard scrabbling sounds close to the high wall, Asio dropping to catch a plump rat which had lived with others about the cottage garden. The rats were attracted to peanuts and other food put out to feed the birds and had many tunnels in the earth banks and hedgerows all about.

A mix of rain, hail and sleet had Asio and Hoolet seeking shelter by day in the conifer forest, one of the oldest plantations of the Forestry Commission in England. For two days the bleak weather persisted, the two owls remaining hidden until late at night when rats moved about near the cottage and weir wall, two dying on each night to feed the long eared's.

On the third day high pressure brought sunshine to the Westcountry, the Taw River running high in spate, a torrent of ochre by day, a river filled with sediment, but silver lit by a full moon that night. Asio and Hoolet, well fed now, but still with wanderlust in their veins, flew along a wide forest ride then out into the moonlight, beneath Orion whose three starred belt pointed to the Dog star Sirius, sparkling green and red in the bright sky, pointing also to their route along the Taw river.

The two owls flew side by side, following the river, passing the villages of Umberleigh and Chapelton to reach the town of Barnstaple. Here they crossed over the moonlit rooftops of the ancient market town to where a gilded cockerel on a church tower swung in the wind, pointing to a wooded hillside.

At 3am of the morning Asio and Hoolet flew to perch in a Scots pine at the top of Tutshill Woods, the old tree one of three in the mainly oak and ash woodland on its south facing hill slope. Here the two owls huddled close together, tired but content, watching a fox trot along a narrow pathway below them, to move out across the field which sloped down along the wood edge to a mill leat and stream.

Chapter 2

Winter passed relatively gently in the wooded valley, the weather mainly from a south westerly prevailing wind bringing a mix of rain and shine. At times easterlys blew cold off Exmoor which saw snow, along with nearby Dartmoor, but it did not snow in the valley or on the towns and villages of North Devon.

February came and with it a week of warm weather, spring-like and bringing new nettle growth and the first lesser celandines to shine golden amongst trees and along lane sides and hedgerows. The first small tortoiseshell and brimstone butterflies were on the wing, from hibernation sites in sheds and amongst ivy. On the nearby estuary barely two miles from the valley, wading birds began to leave for northern breeding haunts, the tidal river becoming gradually quieter with their leaving.

Asio and Hoolet, hunting together in the western edge of the wood, as they had been doing for several days, suddenly heard the piercing shriek of hunting tawny owls, Asio receiving a fearsome and sudden buffeting about the head as one of these larger owls launched at him from out of the darkness.

The two long-eareds had been aware of the presence of the tawny owls in a copse close by the woods but until now their paths had not crossed. Now the attack upon Asio, by the larger of the two tawny owls, the female, had him falling sideways in flight as he struck back with his talons only to find the second tawny owl looming above him. The battle was brief, Asio and Hoolet avoiding injury by winging away out from amongst the trees to follow the waterway upstream. The two owls were left unhurt. They could hear the shrill cries of the tawny owls piercing the sylvan darkness behind them as they flew high, out of the valley towards the dark shadowy forest visible before them as they followed the silver waterway below.

Thus it was that Hoolet followed her mate Asio into the dark afforested area known to human locals as Broomhill, the forest silent save for water sounds below. They found themselves over a large stone built house, then a quarry, and the forest opening to a large glade with a field and large pond. The two owls were at King's Acre and here once more they settled on adjoining branches of a forest edge fir tree and began to preen. More than six hundred miles away, more snow fell upon the silent Scottish Ladder Hills but here two long eared owls gazed about then fell asleep, the tawny owls already forgotten.

Chapter 3

It was April. The March Spring Equinox had passed in balmy days of primroses, violets and wood anemones growing where, for some weeks, lesser celandines had formed shining golden carpets all about the broadleaved woods, spinneys and hedgebanks. Within the forest few wildflowers grew, save at the edges where light penetrated and here bloomed the white flowers of wood sorrel, lighting their cushions of bright green shamrock-like leaves.

Asio and Hoolet had regained the weight lost during their journey south from the Scottish Highlands, night hunting here in the Westcountry forest with its rides and lane adjoining being easy. Hail and rain over a few days during January and

February had soaked the fields but done much more good than harm and March had been a sunny, mild month of mostly dry days and nights.

Now, on the day of the April full moon Hoolet was perched on the large stick nest made by crows the previous summer for she and her mate made no nest of their own, choosing to use the old nests of other species, or tree hollows. Hoolet herself had been hatched, one of two young, from eggs laid by their mother, on the ground in brambles. Her mate Asio was one of three young hatched and raised in the old nest of sparrowhawks, but three miles from Hoolet's birthplace in the Ladder Hills forests.

Hoolet was now sitting on two eggs of her own and had begun incubation with the laying of her first egg. Asio was roosting just twenty yards away, watching over his mate and bringing her food from time to time. The eggs, white and elliptical, were less glossy than those of wood pigeons and being only two in number held well to the rather flattish platform of a nest where the crows had raised four young the previous summer.

Occasionally Asio incubated the two eggs, usually at night so that Hoolet could hunt and stretch her wings in flight about the forest and nearby open fields, the two owls getting to know the area of dense woodlands, pasture fields and river as days went by. Few people visited the area.

The local naturalist who owned King's Acre paid occasional daytime visits, making notes of the wildlife and planting some alder buckthorn trees to attract brimstone butterflies to these, their preferred foodplant. At times a farming landowner would poke about to see who might be wandering in the area for sometimes poachers watched the woods and river to see what prizes they might take, for this was a place of red deer and salmon.

It was on the day of the May full moon that Asio found Hoolet standing at the nest edge with two downy, newly hatched owlets, the first long eared owls to see the light of day in the valley for two centuries.

For all of that day Asio and Hoolet perched at the nest, guarding their young and as night fell Asio hooted deep and low with a sound like someone blowing across the neck of an empty glass bottle, then he flew to hunt for the nestlings first meal.

On the 25th day from hatching the two young long eared owls left the nest to fly out onto the grassy hillside overlooking King's Acre. They flew strongly, following Asio and Hoolet onto the foxglove covered earth bank adjoining the forest, learning to hunt with their parents as is the way of owls.

It was on Midsummer's night that the naturalist landowner visited the site following a long day's work at his other larger landownership a few miles distant. He leaned on the gateway of King's Acre by a stone built linhay, hearing and watching the long eared owls as they hunted in the swiftly gathering darkness. Later in his notebook he wrote:

"Four long eared owls hunting about King's Acre, a successful outcome to this exciting find. This is my 3rd nesting pair to raise young in North Devon since 1972 when I found eggs and the two adults at Shearford Lane, Barnstaple whilst clearing the footpath route"…

Trevor Beer's FIVE OWLS

5

Flammeus & Shade
A Tale of Short-eared Owls

Chapter 1

April morning sunshine breaking through the mist and a richly orange comma butterfly flew from an old orchard and along a flooded ditch or rhyne in the Somerset Levels country. The butterfly had gone into hibernation as an adult insect the previous November, as cold northerly winds brought hail and rain to the countryside. Eggs laid in July on the upper surface of stinging nettle leaves had hatched to produce larva, then August pupa which became September adults of the dark form of comma.

The insect had hibernated in a hollow of a pollarded willow and now, stimulated by the sun's warmth, flew as the first of its kind to be on the wing on this fine spring day. By mid morning other commas were on the move, their ragged edged wings carrying them in swift flight across the wild marsh country as chiff chaff song merged with that of resident blackbirds, robins and a song thrush. The chiff chaffs were the first summering migrant birds to arrive back from Africa to breed, singing three weeks before the willow warblers, here before the first swallows even, though a few of that species were now arriving in the Westcountry.

The distant sound of a cuckoo calling had some of the small song birds perching about in agitation on tree and shrub branches, a 'meadow pipit cuckoo' which had flown from

France to England two days before, to seek out a mate who would lay in the nests of meadow pipits hereabouts.

The cuckoo calls came nearer and soon the bird could be seen flying low in hedge hopping flight, to alight on a fence erected the previous autumn. The bird, sparrowhawk-like in flight but unmistakable when perched, scanned the marshy area for host species for its mate's eggs but finding none, called its 'cuckoo' calls then flew on across the grassland.

Two black-centred, pale yellow eyes, highlighted by a ring of smokey black feathers, gazed at the cuckoo as it flew overhead. Flammeus the short-eared owl stretched up tall and slender, watching the cuckoo out of sight and he clicked the razor sharp hooked beak hidden amongst pale buff and grey feathers below his facial discs.

Then launching himself from the ground where he had night roosted amongst jointed rush and yellow flag leaves he flew on long wings, using up-currents in the wind to glide up and over a farmer in noiseless flight.

The farmer was planting trees along the new fence line, needing the immediacy of the fence but wanting to screen it with hawthorn and blackthorn for he loved the look of dense hedgerows and the wildlife they supported. Now he paused, spade in hand as the owl flew over him, knowing it was a short-eared, and noting the barring on the wings and tail and the dark carpal patches clearly visible at the angle of the leading edges of the owl's underwings. He grinned as he saw the owl glide then drop suddenly to grab prey, typical of this species hunting technique as he knew from numerous sightings over several years.

During the winter he had watched as many as five short-eared owls hunting over his land during bleak days, knowing their numbers were augmented by migrants from the Continent at that time. The owl he now watched was one of a few residents, he knew. They nested and bred here on the marshes though he kept quiet about it rather than have them pressured or persecuted, which even the well-meaning can unintentionally do.

Flammeus loved this wild mix of open moorland and marsh with its rough grasses and now he glided just a foot or two above the grass on slightly upraised wings. He had eaten the field vole he had just killed and was enjoying his bouncy flight which, totally silent, gave his prey no warning.

Now the voles would soon be producing about five voles each, every seven weeks, the offspring themselves able to breed at six weeks. Apart from attempting to hide from predators, prolific breeding is the creatures main mode of defending its numbers and existence, with every four or five years the voles reaching plague proportions. This means a consequent rise in owl breeding success and two years before had resulted in Flammeus and four other owlets hatching on a warm summer's day.

Now he caught and ate another vole then flew up high over his territory, to suddenly boom out his call, a rapid, panting, 'po-po-po-po', which the farmer heard quite clearly. He stopped digging again, wiping his sweating brow with a red and white spotted handkerchief as Flammeus called again. The sound reminded the farmer of the noise made by the steam train puffing up the incline out of Taunton during his days in the

RAF, before the time of Beeching's 'Axe', and then the diesel engine.

He sighed. He could watch the owls and other wildlife all day. He looked across to the post where he'd hung his knapsack with his lunch and binocular. No, must get the trees in the ground. Rain in the offing and that would water them in nicely. Time to bird watch later, in the sunset time, or while having his lunch.

'Po-po-po-po'. Flammeus called again, clapping his wings beneath his body like a nightjar, but behind his tail more, and then he plummeted several feet earthwards, to glide again then repeat the performance.

At the grassland edge where it joined heather moorland a female short-eared owl perched on a pollarded willow her body held in almost horizontal stance. She was Shade, one of eight young in a brood, of the same year as Flammeus, a time when the vole plague's bountiful food supply has produced record numbers of owls in response.

Some owls had laid as many as 10 eggs to a clutch and others had raised two broods in the season but the abundance of prey and predator was typically short lived. Over crowding brought about a cessation in vole breeding and that coupled with the heavy predation, by foxes, stoats, weasels, and other birds of prey as well as the owls, had meant a sudden dispersal of most predators as competition for the remaining food became tougher.

But as ever is the case a few had remained about. Shade had become restless from being with her family, watching them fly seawards where the dunes and marshes of Bridgwater Bay and Blue Anchor beckoned them home.

She had wintered at King's Sedge Moor, thriving there and around Westonzoyland for food for a fewer predators remained plentiful. The next summer she had found a mate but he had been struck by a vehicle while flying low along a country lane and had fallen dying into a ditch. Shade searched for many days which became weeks but found no sign of him as she wandered the countryside. She spent the next mild autumn and winter in the King's Sedge Moor countryside then in the March flew south to Muchelney where some urge deep within her called her westwards to West Sedge Moor.

Here Shade had wandered between the Parrett and the Tone Rivers, feeding on mice and voles, seeing none of her kind save for little owls who were about by day. But then on a day when primroses lit the lanes and hedges with pale colour and swallows flew inland from the shores which had been her home two years before, she had heard the excited, 'po-po-po-po' of another such as she and had perched watching Flammeus in his hopeful display flight.

Shade launched herself from her willow tree perch, flying rapidly, low over the rough grassland, every fibre of her being eager for the company of another short-eared owl, responding to the primitive urges that have kept wild creatures living down through millions of years.

Flammeus, rising high to boom out his song yet again, twisted his wings downwards and clapping them together once more, saw an owl below him and he called aloud, calling to her and to the empty air no longer.

"Well blessed be!" The farmer, who could not resist glancing occasionally skywards on hearing the owl calling, had caught sight of Flammeus, and then the second owl in rapid flight below him. He watched awestruck as the lower owl suddenly checked in flight to wing upwards, the two birds flying together high above him in a wide circle.

Shade half closed her wings dropping sharply earthwards then gliding to perch on a post in the fence line. Flammeus followed her, perching first on the next post, then dropping swiftly to the ground to immediately catch a field vole. Holding it firmly he flew back to his perch then leaving the prey upon the post top he flew a further post distant and watched the other owl.

Shade lifted her ear tufts towards him, raising her body to its full height, standing tall, then gradually she lowered to the horizontal position. Still Flammeus waited and then Shade was suddenly on the prey post, to carry the vole to the ground and there she ate it.

"Glory be", chuckled the farmer. "He's taken her out for a meal already, now that's fast work".

Chapter 2

Flammeus and Shade were mated. April passed by, a month of showers and sunshine, the two owls finding shelter when needed beneath a gorse brake left by the farmer whose wife made country wine from the flowers. Once the gorse had been used as fodder for cattle in winter, and then to help fuel and old Boddley kitchen range until an Aga cooker took its place.

Now the gorse shone its rich gold flowers to brighten the

marshes, to play host to green hairstreak butterflies and a pair of linnets who had just built a nest within its safe, spiky vegetation.

In a grassy hollow, well sheltered from prevailing winds by the gorse Shade laid five white eggs at two day intervals, beginning to incubate from the first laid. This was to ensure that the eggs would hatch at two day intervals also, then with the food supply judged correctly there would be enough for the whole family. With Flammeus the sole provider at this critical time, feeding Shade throughout the incubation of four weeks, if they were to over estimate the food availability only the youngest should die. This strategy of the short-eared owls, born of millions of years of nature's wisdom, says it is better to raise a few healthy young than many weak ones. It is the wisdom of survival.

From the vantage point of his parked vehicle the farmer, oft times accompanied by his wife, watched Flammeus busily hunting the marshes, seeing that no-one went onto the land to harm the owls. Twice roe deer strayed close to the gorse brake but they were only passing through and a few rapid wing-clapping dives from Flammeus about their heads had them trotting away with no damage done.

With all chicks hatched and hungry the task of hunting grew busier for Flammeus but the weather was kind in the main and with Shade tearing up the food and feeding them they grew swiftly, their down changing from white to grey. Then as they became feathered and larger one vole became one mouthful for one owl, Shade joining Flammeus in the hunting.

Pellets of indigestible food lay scattered about and on the 21st day of fledging the young owls were strong, moving about with much wing flapping. On the 23rd day, during a six hour period watched for much of the time by the farmer and his wife, all five young lifted from the grasses to quarter the field low flying but strong, with the two adults.

"I think a drop of gorse wine to celebrate, don't you agree dear". The farmer's wife put her arm about her husband.

"Can't think of a better reason m'dear. Let's leave them be, they look fit and happy to me".

Epilogue
Owls in Folklore

Worldwide it is thought owls are birds of superstition, magic and wisdom. There is a tendency for humans to attribute strange powers and ill omen to some night creatures and thus owls have had their unfair share of such prejudices when they can truly be said to be either beneficial to mankind, or 'neutral' in the sense they are not harmful in any way.
Even Shakespeare was a bit of a misery where owls and owlets were concerned, using the birds' more ominous symbolism, and sadly such beliefs die hard.

But as creatures of the night with remarkable eyesight they were further persecuted in that their eggs were taken, cooked and powdered then used in potions to improve our own eyesight. And owl broth was also made and used to cure whooping cough, more sympathetic magic, the owl's hooting call removing the hooting cough!

The Little owl is the owl of wisdom, the owl sacred to Athene, goddess of wisdom. The bird was held in great reverence and as Athene was also renowned for her calm and moderate ways, so the little owl was thought to cure madness, drunkenness and epilepsy. The poor birds just could not win.

In some parts the short-eared owl is known as the Pilot Owl, as in winter when some arrived as migrants, along with woodcock, they were considered to be guiding that lovely wader to our shores.

Oddly the Athenians who so loved the little owl were anti the long-eared owl, using its name Otus as a term of derision for idiots and simpletons. It was thought that if you walked around a long-eared owl it would turn its head to follow your movement about it until it wrung its own neck.

Today, hopefully, all our owls are much loved.